Also available in this series

CANDLEMAKING
JEWELLERY
POTTERY
APPLIQUE
FRAMING
SOFT TOYS Book 1
MACRAME
CROCHET
RUGMAKING
WEAVING
MORE SOFT TOYS
COUNTRY CRAFTS
THE ART OF DRIED AND PRESSED FLOWERS
FILOGRAPHY
BARGELLO
FURNITURE MAKING
CHILDREN'S CLOTHES
GIFTS

METRIC CONVERSION TABLE		
INCHES		MILLIMETRES
1/4	=	6
1/2	=	13
3/4	=	19
1	=	25
2	=	51
3	=	76
4	=	102
5	=	127
6	=	152
7	=	178
8	=	203
9	=	229
10	=	254

home decoration

ISABEL HUNT

illustrated by Marilyn Day
photography by Richard Sharpe Studios

PAN BOOKS LTD
LONDON AND SYDNEY

ACKNOWLEDGEMENTS
The publishers wish to express their gratitude to the following
for their help in supplying designs and materials:
Dralon Information Bureau: pages 8–9. Portways Ltd.,
for original design of pouffe: pages 8–9. M & F Products
Ltd.: pages 12–14. Belinda Black: pages 16–17. The Flower House,
Fulham Road, London, S.W.10.: pages 24–25. Hobby Horse
Ltd., Langton Street, London, S.W.10.: pages 50–51.
Nairn Dunbar Ltd.: pages 66–67. Berger Paints (Wall
Patterns) Ltd.: pages 76–79. Dralon International Ltd.:
pages 88–91.

First published 1974 by Sampson Low
This edition published 1975 by Pan Books Ltd,
Cavaye Place, London SW10 9PG

 © Intercontinental Book Productions

Printed in Spain
ISBN 0 330 24485 X

CONTENTS

INTRODUCTION

Which one of us doesn't like to have beautiful things in our homes? But increasingly, which one of us can afford to buy, even some of the elegant and tempting things so tastefully displayed in expensive shops and glossy magazines?

There is no reason, however, why such things, and many more too, should not be made at home and often at very minimal expense. But even putting aside the cost factor, important though it is, there is something very satisfying for both men and women to actually make something themselves that fits their particular life style as it enhances the appearance of their home.

In this book we have proved that anybody can become a handyman or woman, and make things they will be proud of! There are ideas for just about every room in the house—drawing room, kitchen, hall, bathroom, bedroom, nursery, even a patio area—and the instructions for making or implementing them are clear and explicit. Of course we have included things that all women appreciate a little professional advice about, such as making unusual patchwork cushions, original curtain ideas, round and oval tablecloths that really fit the tables, how to turn your bed into a romantic four-poster, lovely trimming ideas to give new life to towels and bed linen, but in addition there are some really unusual ideas to make your home rather special and unique. Things like masking a window to change its uniform shape, creating a raised area in a room,

effective use of mirrors and transforming an old junky bookcase into an unusual display cabinet. Try out a few of these projects and see the difference they make to your home.

We recommend you to follow our easy step-by-step illustrated instructions, particularly if you are not yet an experienced 'do-it-yourselfer'. But feel free to experiment as well, to adapt designs and use different materials to suit your home and personality. Practise a few techniques before embarking on anything too ambitious and start new projects only when you have lots of time to tackle them. Read the introductions to each item too, as they often include time and labour-saving hints or advice about method and materials.

The You Will Need column on the first page of each project lists materials needed for making that item. Space has often made it impossible to include equipment such as scissors, bowls and so on. However these are things that will be close at hand in every home and a read through the instructions will quickly determine all the 'extras' you need. Collect everything together before you begin so you are not halfway through making something, when you discover you are missing essential equipment.

We are confident that this book will lead you on to making all sorts of original, exciting things for your home, so take your confidence in both hands and start right away. You will be surprised at the professional results of your labours.

Seating For Six

This gigantic pouffe will be a great talking, as well as seating point! Shaped in segments, we have made it to resemble a huge orange, but choose a colour that suits your room. To give you an idea of how much space you need, it measures 60 in. across and is approximately 18 in. deep. If that seems too large why not scale it down to suit the space you have. If room permits, however, it really is a dramatic piece of furniture and useful too!

YOU WILL NEED:
6 in. thick foamed polystyrene cut into a circle 54 in. in diameter
Matching synthetic thread
60 lb. ICI Terylene P3 filling or similar stuffing
2 plywood discs, 4 in. diameter
Upholstery skewer

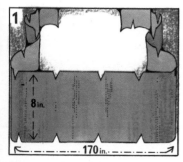

Make up a strip in fabric 8×170 in. If using corduroy, cord must be set vertical. Cut 1 in. deep notches every 6 in. top and bottom.

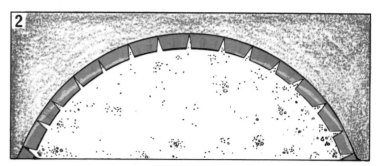

Join ends to form a circle. Place around plinth (i.e. polystyrene circle) and glue down top and bottom overlap with impact adhesive. The notches will open out so fabric lies flat.

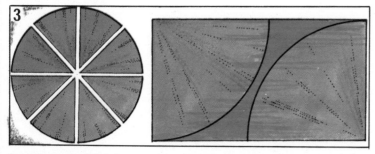

Cut 16 panels of fabric to make into 2 circles. The sides of each panel should be 34 in. long with a 45° angle between them. Cut the remaining side in an arc. Make sure the grain of the fabric runs the same way in all the panels.

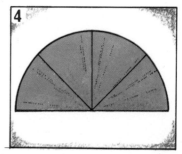

Right sides fabric together join panels in pairs with 2 in. seams on each panel. (Two pairs form $\frac{1}{2}$ a circle.)

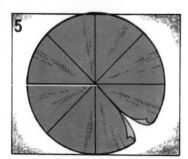

Join 4 pairs to make complete circle. Repeat for second circle, but leave one pair unstitched to allow for stuffing.

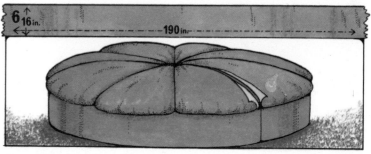

Cut widths of fabric 16 in. deep and join to make a border 190 in. long. (The grain of corduroy should be set vertical in all pieces.) Attach to top and bottom circles, using synthetic thread. Double stitch all seams for strength.

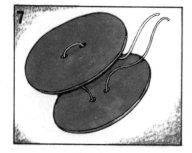

Fill the cushion. Drill two holes $\frac{1}{8}$ in. wide either side of centre of each plywood disc. Thread through loops of string.

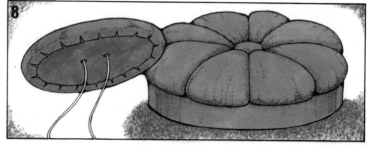

Cover discs with wadding and fabric. Attach cord to upholstery skewer and thread each disc through centre, opposite sides of pouffe. Tie in middle with slip knot and pull to adjust tension. Tie with firm knot. Slip stitch opening. Rest pouffe on plinth.

In the Picture

Give character to a modern window by masking it with a hardboard frame. You can either paint it to tone in with the room's colour scheme, or cover it with wallpaper to match the walls as in our picture. Both are equally effective, but if you choose to cover the frame with wallpaper avoid exaggerated curves on the design as these make it difficult to get the paper flat. Use this idea to hide old curtain track or the roller of a blind, or just to soften the outline of a regimentally square frame. For each window you will need three strips of hardboard about 9 in. wide. The one for the top of the window should overlap by 6 in. on each side. The other two pieces should equal the sides of the window.

YOU WILL NEED:
Sheets of hardboard
(see introduction for
measurements)
Pad saw
Glasspaper
Spirit level
Pencil
Straight edge rule
Contact adhesive
Paint or wallpaper

1

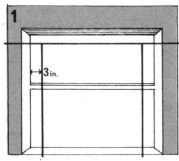

Cut the three strips of hardboard to fit the window (see introduction). Hardboard should not cover more than 3 in. of window pane.

2

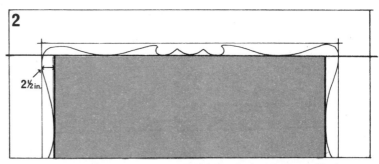

Place strips on floor as they will be fixed on window. Mark your design on top strip and one of sides. (Curves should not be deeper than 2½ in.) Use a measure to mark pattern in regular intervals. Use side piece as a template and mark other side.

3

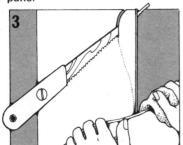

Using pad saw, cut out patterns on all pieces. Glasspaper all cut edges to make them smooth.

4

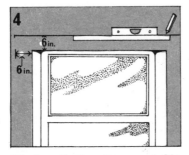

Mark wall 6 in. above and 6 in. either side of window. Use a spirit level and straight edge rule for accuracy.

5

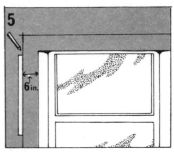

Repeat down 1 side of window to mark positions of side strip. Transfer exact measurements to the other side.

6

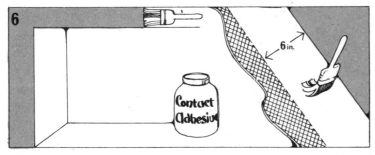

Make sure wall is very clean and dry, then smear a thin film of contact adhesive within your marked guidelines. Do the same on wrong sides of the cut hardboard strips.

7

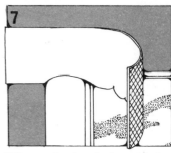

When adhesive is 'touch' dry, fix top strip in place. Start at 1 corner, use only hand pressure and keep strictly to your lines.

8

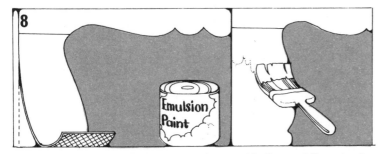

Line up outer edges of side pieces along guide lines whilst pressing down. When all the strips are in place, leave until set. Then prime with thinned emulsion paint. When dry paint in the chosen colour.

9

If covering with wallpaper, snip paper to go round curves in design. Apply as you would to the wall.

Lamps and Lampshades

Covering your own lampshades is one sure way of bringing your particular personal touch into a room. A quick and easy way too, and far cheaper than buying lampshades from a shop. The shapes of frames on the market are endless, the choice is yours and none of them is hard to cover. Remember to buy a little extra fabric when buying for curtains, so you can cover a lampshade to match. Or for something really easy— try our extra quick idea of merely draping lacy fabric over a tiffany-type frame. Couldn't be simpler—but the effect is floating and romantic. Buy plastic coated frames whenever possible as these are washable and do not rust. Alternatively paint untreated metal frames with quick drying white enamel paint. Lamp bases are an even more expensive item, but there are endless things you can use to make them. Attractively shaped bottles are a great favourite, but we give instructions here for converting a wooden log into a lamp base. There's no way it will topple over.

YOU WILL NEED:
Lampshade frames (we give instructions for drum, petal and tiffany shapes, but they can be adapted to most shapes)
Fabric for covering (amount depends on size of frame—see instructions for measuring)
Matching thread
Matching bias binding
For drum shape—parchment to fit (see instructions for measuring)
Glue for fabric
For lamp base:
Log of wood (ours was approximately 11 in. diameter and 9 in. tall)
Lampholder attachment
Lighting flex
Clear Polyurethane varnish
Drill

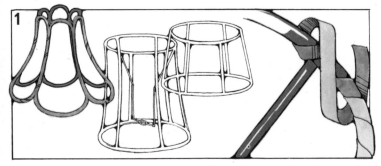

1 Whatever the shape of frame it must be bound to provide a foundation for stitching on the covering. Use $\frac{1}{2}$ in. bias binding. Anchor to frame with glue, then bind tightly round rings and struts, using a figure of eight action where they meet. Glue end.

2 Choose a colour binding that blends with fabric covering. Tape tightly or it will move when covering is attached.

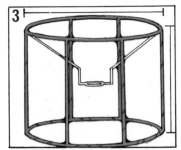

3 Drum shade: this is one of the easiest to cover. Bind as described in No. 1. Measure circumference and height.

4 Cut a piece of imitation parchment $\frac{1}{2}$ in. bigger each way, and a piece of fabric 1 in. wider and 3 in. deeper.

5 Place parchment on wrong side of fabric and turn over top and bottom surplus. Glue these to hold in place.

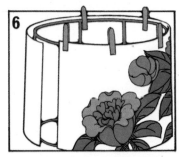

6 When dry, wrap shade round frame. Use clothes pegs to hold in place.

7 Tuck one side in between parchment and fabric of other side. Turn in $\frac{1}{2}$ in. of fabric; oversew edge with matching thread.

8 Stitch shade to frame at top and bottom of struts—where they meet the ring of frame.

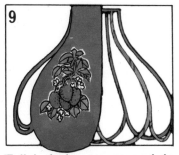

9 'Tulip' shades are covered in sections. Bind frame. Centre a motif in fabric on each panel. Cut out with 1 in. margin all round.

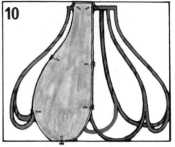

10 Take 2 pieces of fabric, right sides together and pin to frame on one section. Place pins in 4 corners first, then in centre of struts.

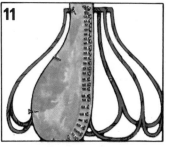

11 Pin down struts from centre pin then pin up to the top. Pull fabric taut all the time and adjust pins if necessary.

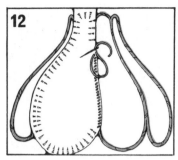

12 Oversew through both thicknesses of fabric down righthand strut. Cut off surplus fabric close to stitch line.

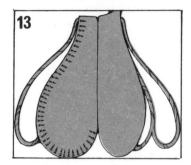

13 Peel open top layer of fabric by removing and replacing one pin at a time. Leave bottom layer pinned taut to frame.

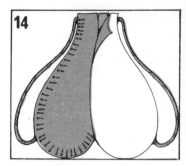

14 Place 3rd panel of fabric over 2nd panel. Pin and oversew double thickness of fabric to frame as before. Trim surplus.

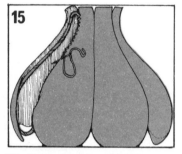

15 Work round frame in this way. When you reach end, oversew first panel to left hand strut and trim surplus turnings.

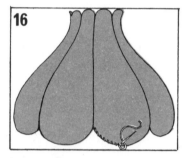

16 Turn under edge of last panel and neatly oversew this to first panel. Stitch all panels on top and bottom of frame.

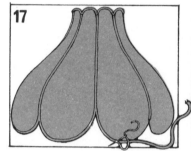

17 Seams can be covered with bias binding. Pick a colour used in fabric and hem down over struts using tiny stitches.

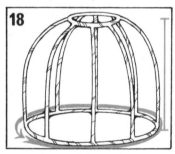

18 Tiffany shades can be covered in 2 ways. Measure overall height of struts and circumference of base of shade.

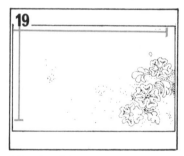

19 Allowing 2 in. extra on measurements cut a square or rectangle using soft, non-bulky material. Bind frame.

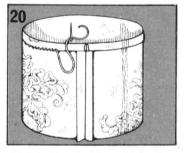

20 Right sides inside, stitch along 'height' sides to make a tube. Turn under and stitch hem at top leaving a small opening.

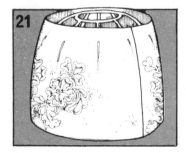

21 Turn tube right side out and pull over frame; line seam over a strut where it will be least obtrusive.

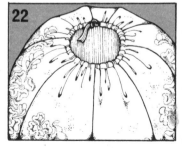

22 Thread $\frac{1}{4}$ in. elastic through top hem. Pull up so hole is about 2 in. diameter. Tie ends of elastic and poke back in hem.

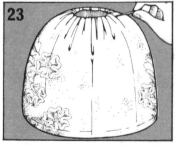

23 Stroke gathers with end of needle to smooth them in place. Turn surplus over rim at bottom. Hem to bound struts.

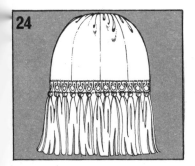

24 Sew on a deep edging of cluny lace or tasselled soft furnishing trimming to the bottom.

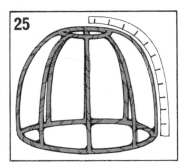

25 An alternative method is a casual 'throw-over' look. Measure height of frame, taking tape to centre of hole and down over a strut.

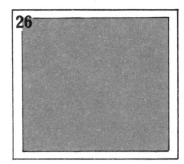

26 Add 6 in. then double total measurement and cut a square of fabric. Lace or flimsy fabric is the most effective.

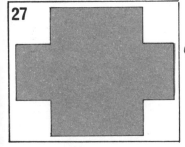

27 Measure and cut out a 6 in. square at each corner. This prevents an extra long drop at the corners.

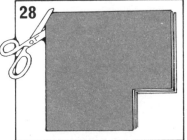

28 Find centre of fabric by folding in 4 and cut out 1 in. wide hole just big enough to thread lamp fitting through.

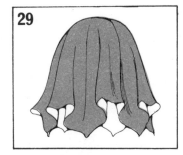

29 Make small hems on all cut edges if fabric frays. Attach ric-rac or similar braid round edges. Place over frame.

30 Lamp bases can be made from all sorts of things—bottles are a particular favourite. General rule to follow is that the shade should be wider than the base so as to give a balanced look and in order not to block light from the bulb.

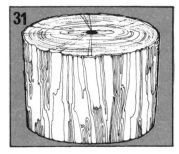

31 Our photograph shows a lamp base made from a log of wood. Select log and drill hole right through centre to take flex.

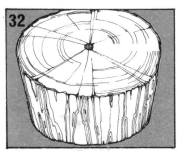

32 Drill a groove from one side to centre of base for flex to sit in so wood stands level.

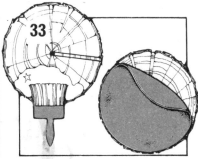

33 Leave bark on and seal ends with polyurethane. Cover base with felt or baize to avoid it scratching surfaces.

34 Screw in lampholder and attach shade.

15

Hang-ups with Off-cuts

A pictorial montage out of carpet remnants is a novel and exciting way of putting those off-cuts from fitted carpets to use, instead of pushing them into a polythene bag and thrusting them into a far corner of a cupboard! But don't despair— it isn't an idea only for those with fitted carpets! Look out for off-cuts in sales which usually sell quite cheaply, but avoid acrylics or loosely woven piles which reveal the backing.

The skill here lies in matching textures and colours, whilst keeping your design very classic and simple. Remember carpet frays, but it is easy to cut and handle in small pieces.

We gave our picture a really professional finish, by making it to fit one of the standard aluminium picture framing kits available from big stores. They are easy to use, but obviously you must make sure you make your picture to fit the size of the assembled frame.

YOU WILL NEED:
3 different coloured off-cuts of carpets
Sharp trimming knife
Latex adhesive and spreader
Small hammer
Sheet of $\frac{1}{4}$ in. plywood to fit frame
Very stiff card, same size as plywood
Nail file
1 aluminium picture framing kit or double glazing gasket or draught excluder to fit round picture.

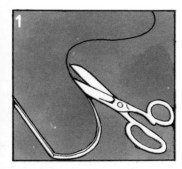

Copy the pattern from our picture (left) draw on to the stiff card. Cut card into 3 templates.

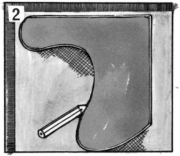

Place templates on back of each piece of carpet. Draw round with soft pencil, in case template slips while cutting.

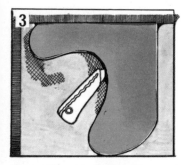

Score through back of carpet with sharp knife around template. Remove template and cut through carpet backing along score line.

When backing is cut through, gently pull pile apart. Try not to fray edge of pattern piece.

Repeat with all pieces of carpet. Put 3 pieces together to check fit. (Small discrepancies can be filled later.)

Apply adhesive to back of carpet and plywood. Let it partially dry for good adhesion and press carpet into place. Avoid excess of adhesive as this is difficult to remove from pile.

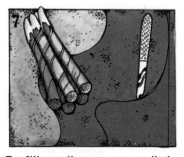

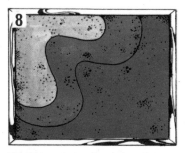

To fill small gaps, put a little adhesive on end of few loose tufts. Part carpet 'joins' and push tufts in with a nailfile.

Fit picture into aluminium frame, following instructions on kit.

Alternatively, trim edge of plywood with channeled plastic such as double glazing gasket or draught excluder.

'Antique' Display Case

Nearly every junk shop has a collection of seemingly ugly and not very useful bookcases, which are still very cheap to buy. Many of them don't show off books to advantage, but with a little imagination they can be turned into an elegant display cabinet which looks good in any drawing room setting. Look out for any bookcases for this project, although one set off the ground with short legs is probably the best type. One good thing, there is no need to strip off the layers of old paint or varnish that the bookcase has probably collected over the years. So the labour involved is really minimal, and the result is enviable!

YOU WILL NEED:
Old bookcase
Tubes of thick gold paint (Goldfinger)
Dark Green felt or Fablon
Gold coloured velvet-type fabric
1 in. thick foam
Gold curtain braid
Brass stud nails
Impact adhesive
(Amounts of material will depend on the size of the bookcase.)

Wipe the bookcase over with a damp cloth. Surface does not need to be smooth—a few blemishes enhance appearance.

Allow to dry, then cover all visible external surfaces, except for shelves, with thick gold paint. Apply thickly, but do not try to achieve smooth finish—this is not necessary.

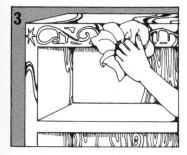

Leave to dry, then rub over with a soft cloth, to slightly 'polish' the surface.

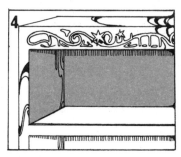

Cut pieces of felt or Fablon to fit all inside walls. Stick down firmly, making sure they fit exactly. Trim if necessary.

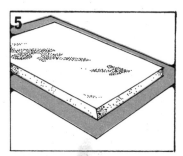

Cut foam to fit shelves exactly. Cut velvety fabric to cover top and sides of foam, allowing an extra 3 in. all round.

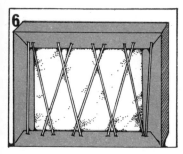

Place fabric on top of foam. Turn over and glue down turnings or secure by stitching across back of pad.

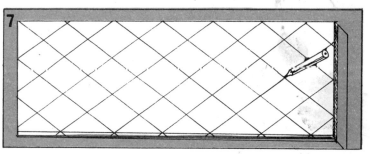

On a piece of paper the same size as the top of the pad, mark out places of 'buttons' by drawing diagonal lines either way as shown. Buttons will come at points where lines cross. Lay paper on top of pad, and mark button points *only* on to pad.

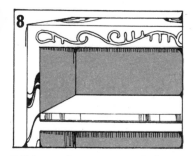

Stick pads on to shelves—fabric side up.

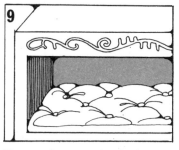

Hammer brass stud nails through to shelf on marked points to achieve a 'buttoned' effect.

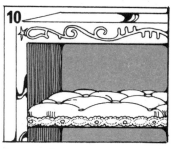

Cut gold trimming the same length as shelf. Nail along front of shelf using brass stud nails.

Please be Seated

It's easy to add a new dimension to a close carpeted room by carrying the carpet up and over a simply constructed raised area. Scatter a few cushions around and you have a delightfully informal, but extremely economical, sitting area which could easily double as an overnight guest bed. We suggest you make it 24 inches wide, 12 inches high and as long as you like; (our instructions are for 8 foot long). By being clever—or perhaps crafty is a better word as it is no more difficult to construct—you could make the top hinged, so you have a wealth of extra storage space, cunningly concealed beneath a smoothly carpeted exterior!

YOU WILL NEED:
16 ft. timber battens
3×1 in.
18 No. 10 woodscrews and wallplugs
2 dozen No. 8 woodscrews and wallplugs
$\frac{3}{4}$ in. blockboard 10 ft. ×12 in.
$\frac{3}{4}$ in. blockboard 8 ft. ×24 in.
10 ft. timber battens 2×2 in.
Saw and wood chisel
Spirit level . Drill
Carpet tacks or fixing strips
Foam (optional)
8 ft.×24 in.×12 in.
Carpet to fit (see instructions)
If top is to be hinged, you will also need:
3 small door hinges
8 ft.×2 in.×1 in. timber batten
Latex adhesive.

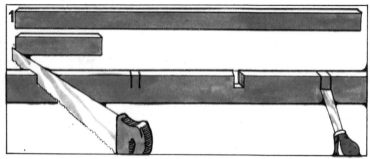

Saw 10 ft. ×3 in. ×1 in. batten into 23¼ in. and 8 ft. lengths. Notch 8 ft. batten at 2 ft. intervals—i.e. make 2 saw cuts 1½ in. deep and ¾ in. wide. Chop out with a wood chisel.

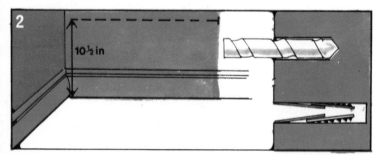

Measure 10½ in. up wall and mark screw holes 18 in. apart on wall to take long batten. Drill and plug wall.

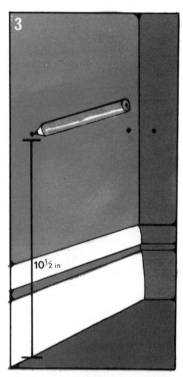

Mark screw holes on wall to take short batten, 10½ in. up from floor, 6 in. apart.

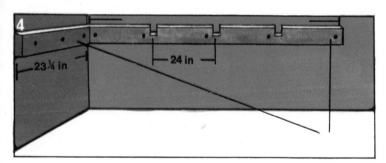

Screw both battens to wall using a spirit level. Use 2½ in. No. 10 woodscrews.

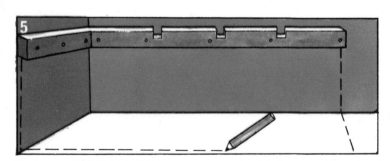

Mark screw holes in floor to correspond with long wall, and at opposite end to side wall. Drill and plug if necessary.

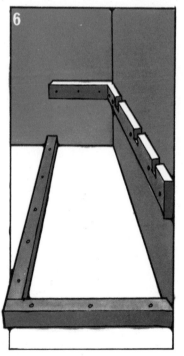

Cut 2 in. square timber battens into 8 ft. and 23¼ in. lengths. Screw to floor in marked holes.

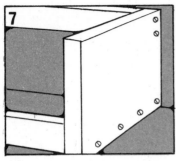

Cut a panel of blockboard 23¼ × 12 in. Screw to end floor batten and edge of long wall batten using 1¾ in. No. 8 woodscrew.

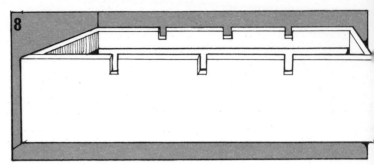

Cut front blockboard panel, 8 ft. × 12 in. Cut 3 in. deep notches to correspond with those in wall batten.

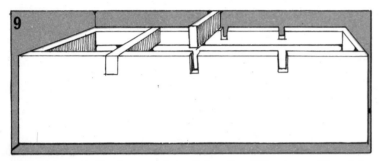

Saw 3 × 1 in. timber battens into 3 lengths 24 in. long. Glue into notches in batten and panel and nail in place with 1½ in. oval nails.

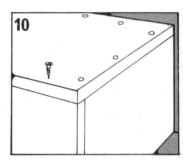

Cut top from ¾ in. blockboard to fit flush with front and end. Screw to wall battens and panels using No. 8 woodscrews.

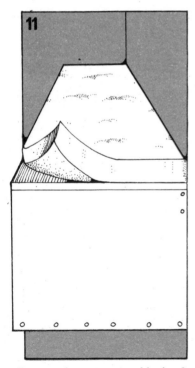

For a soft seat, cut a block of plastic foam to fit on top. Glue in place.

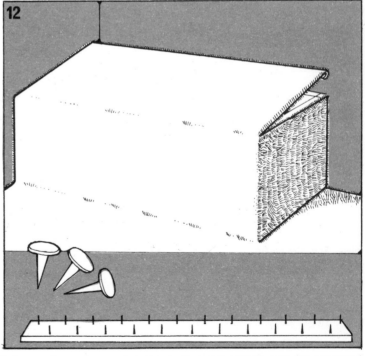

Cut carpet as shown, leaving a 'tongue' which can be wrapped round the end. Secure it with carpet tacks or proprietary gripper strips as used on stair carpet. Fixing points are the unit/floor angle, just underneath the top and along the walls.

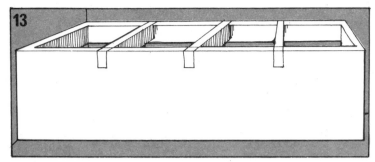

13

If you wish the top of the box can be hinged to give access to space below for storage. Make framework as before and attach side and front panel.

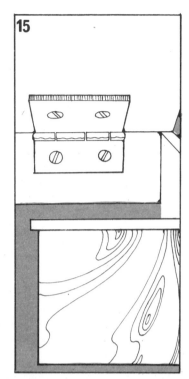

15

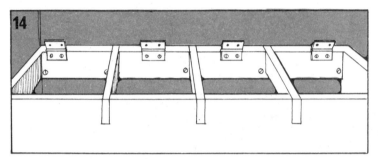

14

Screw on door hinges to edge of back wall batten, 2 ft. apart. (Do not line up screw holes with previous ones or the wood will be weakened.)

Screw free side of door hinges to top of frame. When top is lowered it overlaps front to give a lifting grip.

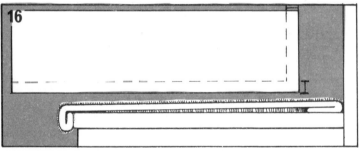

16

Cut a separate piece of carpet for top of box making it approx. 3 in. deeper (from wall to front) and 1½ in. wider. Turn under 1½ in. and tack along back against wall. Wrap remainder under excess top lip only and secure with tacks or adhesive.

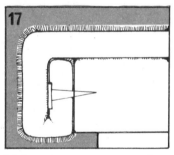

17

Make sure carpet goes to front of frame *only* or lid will not close properly.

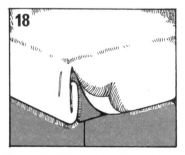

18

Using a latex adhesive, glue carpet to sides of lid only. (This will stop it fraying.)

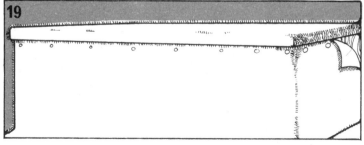

19

Cut remainder of carpet to come level with the top and sides of frame. Glue and tack in place.

The Charm of Flowers

There is hardly a room in the house which does not look better for a vase of flowers. Whether the arrangement be large and dramatic or small and delicate, there is a place and a purpose for it in the home—to liven up a dull corner, to act as a charming centre piece for a dinner table or to cheer up a meal tray for an invalid, to name only a few. There is simply no substitute for the freshness and beauty of flowers, so learn to arrange them to their greatest advantage so you do them justice, and they look their best for you. One point to remember when planning centre piece arrangements for the dinner table, make sure they are low enough for guests to see over!

YOU WILL NEED:
Fresh cut flowers—choose those in season
Assorted vases
Holding material such as Oasis or Florapac

Cut the stems of bought flowers on the slant to open up as much stem as possible. Slash rose stems upwards as well and crush thick woody stems, such as lilac, with a hammer.

Steep all cut and picked flowers in cold water, two-thirds up the stem, for 1½ hours before arranging.

Crumble holding material and pack in vase. Or cut into a shape to fit the vase. Saturate with water before use.

Remove all leaves and branches which would come below water in the vase. These will rot and make water stagnant.

Start arrangement by forming framework for the basic shape. Tallest stems should be about 1½ times the height of vase.

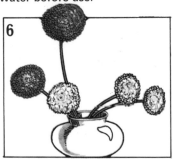

Facing arrangement: put tallest stem at back of vase. Grade shape down to sides and front, using shorter stems.

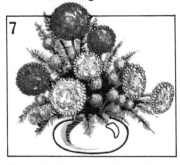

Then build upwards and outwards on the basic shape filling in with foliage.

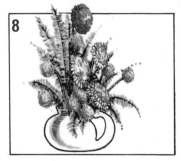

Give this arrangement depth by turning vase round and adding one or two sprays of flowers or foliage at back.

Centre piece: position tallest stem in centre and radiate out from there. Arrange flowers or foliage to cover edges of vase.

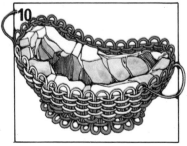

A basket makes an attractive container. Position at its best angle before filling. Line with strong polythene.

A Silver Picture

Add a touch of something unusual to a stark wall with this eye-catching picture. In spite of its sophisticated appearance it is made entirely of oddments such as bits of string and rope, drawing pins, old buttons and buckles and just about anything else you have handy at the time! The 'antique-type' finish is achieved by covering the whole with ordinary kitchen foil, spraying it lightly with paint and rubbing it over quickly with a soft cloth. Easy! Make it in a spare afternoon and hang it up to give your family a bright surprise.

YOU WILL NEED:
Piece of chipboard and cardboard 27 in. square
Oddments of rope and fine string, beads, buttons, drawing pins, old buckles, small pebbles etc.
Glue
Kitchen foil
Brown spray paint
Black paint and brush
2 eyelet screws
Strong cord

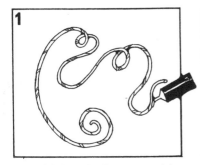

1 Lay chipboard flat on table. Arrange rope, string in a wavy pattern. Glue in place.

2 Cut fine string into varying lengths. Arrange round rope string to make flower stems, leaves etc. Glue in place. Use short lengths of string to make 'veins' in leaves.

3 Push drawing pins into rope in some places to give a different effect. Place pins close together.

4 Add flower and bud details by gluing on buttons, beads, small pebbles, old buckles etc. Allow glue to dry.

5 When completely dry, cover picture with foil. If foil has to be joined, glue edges together securely.

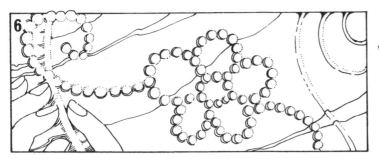

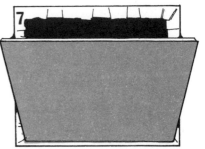

6 Very carefully press foil down around glued objects, so they stand out in high relief, be careful not to tear the foil.

7 Bend foil over back of board and glue down. Cut cardboard slightly smaller than board and glue firmly to back.

8 Spray picture with brown paint. Leave for 30 seconds then carefully rub off with a soft cloth. Some paint will adhere to surface giving an 'antique' finish.

9 Paint the edges of the picture black. Screw in eyelet screw to back on hardboard and hang picture with cord.

It's a Frame-up!

Having pictures framed professionally is usually a very expensive business, yet nothing looks more dismal than a blank wall with no pictures to decorate it. Except, that is, for unframed pictures long since pinned up and with yellowing curling edges. There are lots of ways of doing your own framing which involve very little cost and very little skill. All except one of our ideas avoid the difficult task of mitring corners—an aspect of framing which when badly done, makes it look like a home-made job.

YOU WILL NEED:
(All sizes will depend on size of pictures)
Insulation board
Broomstick or timber dowel, battens and beading
Tin tray
Cake tin
Small blocks of wood
Panel pins
Fixing hooks
Paper glue and impact adhesive
Strong string or wire
Assorted pictures

1

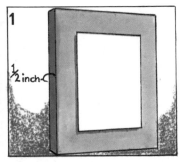

Insulation board makes a light mount. Cut a block of $\frac{1}{2}$ in. board to picture size, plus allowance for a border.

2

Paint the board with three coats of varnish. Mark the area where the picture is to go, and carefully stick it down using a paper glue.

3

Glue a strip of wood to the back. Screw in fixing hooks and attach a length of strong string or wire for hanging.

4

To display posters—cut two lengths of broomstick or timber dowelling slightly longer than width of poster.

6

Weave or plait together several strands of thick wool and tie to the screws. Hang your poster.

5

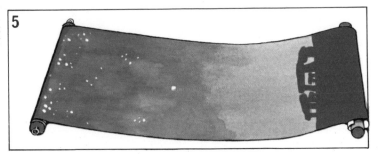

Screw a fixing screw into each end of one piece. Glue top of poster to this and bottom of poster to the other one.

7

A round cake tin makes an unusual frame for a circular picture. De-grease the surface by rubbing with methylated spirits.

8

Spray with aerosol paint using a colour that harmonizes with the picture. (If the tin has an unblemished aluminium-type finish, you may prefer not to paint it.) Glue picture to bottom of tin.

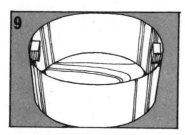

Glue small blocks of wood inside tin near the edge. These correspond with sides of the picture.

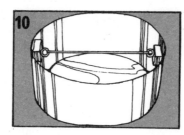

Screw fixing hooks into side pieces of wood and suspend with strong string or wire.

A similar idea is to use an old tin tray. Paint it in a colour that blends with the picture you are framing.

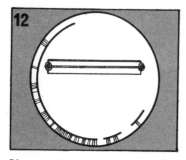

Glue a strip of wood to the back and screw in fixing hooks. Use string or wires to suspend the tray.

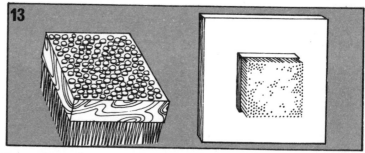

Tiles and plates are sometimes difficult to hang but here is a neat, safe method. Tap several pins through a strip of wood, so one side is studded with sharp points. Glue smooth side to back of tile or plate, using impact adhesive.

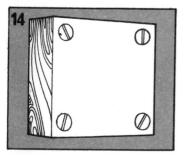

Screw a piece of wood the same size into the wall where you want the subject to hang.

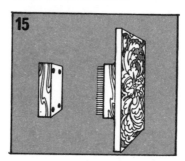

Push the panel pins firmly into the strip of wood on the wall so the plate or tile is securely impaled.

Another idea using insulation board. Cut a block of $\frac{1}{2}$ in. board considerably larger than the picture to be framed.

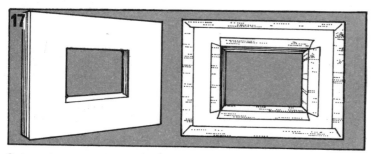

Cut a piece out of the centre the same size as the picture and cover the board with coloured hessian. Stretch this tightly round the board and through the centre hole. Secure at the back with strong glue or small tacks.

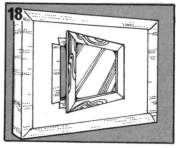

Glue strips of timber batten to edges of picture and glue to back of board over the centre hole.

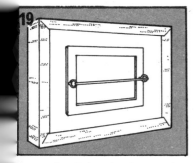

Screw in fixing hooks to the wood either side of the picture and suspend with strong string or wire.

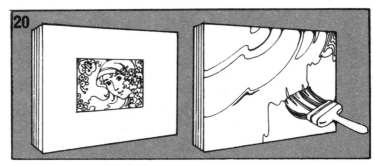

Using insulation board again, cut a block considerably larger than the picture to be framed. Cover with 3 coats of varnish.

Cut a block of board the same size as the picture. Glue the picture to it.

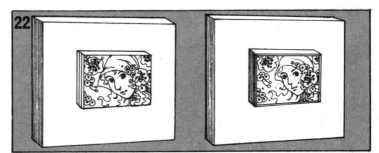

Glue this to the centre of the larger board. Cut 4 pieces of 1 in. flat timber beading to fit the sides of the picture. Glue them to the insulation board with the mounted picture.

Use single channel sliding door track in black plastic to make an effective frame. First mount the picture on a piece of hardboard or strong cardboard.

Cut the track into strips slightly longer than the sides of the mounted picture. Using a mitre block, mitre the corners using a strong craft knife or saw.

Glue the track to the mount with strong glue, taking extra care at the corners.

Patched Together

Patchwork with a difference! No templates or fiddly backing papers are needed to make these super cushions but the results are striking and dramatic! You will need lots of scraps of materials of the same weight, and if they are washable so much the better.

YOU WILL NEED:
¾ yd. 36 in. wide material
(for small inside square)
Several scraps of material
Lining material 17×17 in.
Backing material 17×17 in.
Needle and thread
16 in. zip

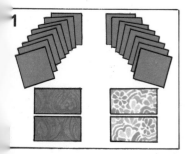

1 Cut 16 1½ in. squares of material in one colour or pattern. Cut 4 strips 3×1 in., two of each colour.

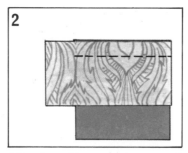

2 Allowing ¼ in. turnings, and right-sides of fabric together machine or backstitch 1 strip to 1 side of the square.

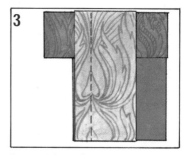

3 Press this strip back and attach a strip of the same material to the first strip in the same way.

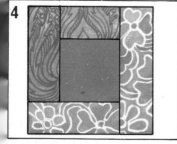

4 Attach remaining two different coloured strips in the same way so that the square is completely surrounded.

5 Cut 4 strips 4×1 in. in two materials. Attach to outside strips in the same way as the first 4, allowing ¼ in. turnings.

6 Cut 4 strips 5×1 in. in two more colours and attach these to complete one square block.

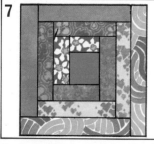

7 Each finished strip in the block is ½ in. wide, with a 1 in. square in the middle. Make 16 squares in the same way. Use the same coloured strips of material for 2 squares each time, so that 8 pairs are the same.

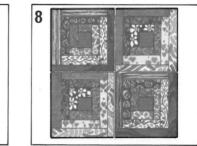

8 Join squares so that pairs of the same material are diagonally opposite each other.

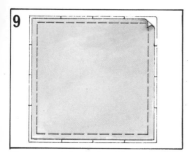

9 Press patchwork. Place lining fabric flat on top (wrong sides together), back stitch round edge so cover is smooth.

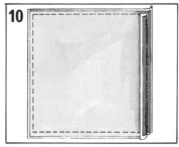

10 Place backing material and patchwork right sides together. Sew along 3 sides. Turn to right side and sew zip along 4th side.

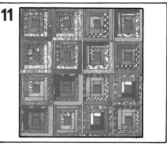

11 Press front and back cover again and insert cushion. Zip up.

On Reflection

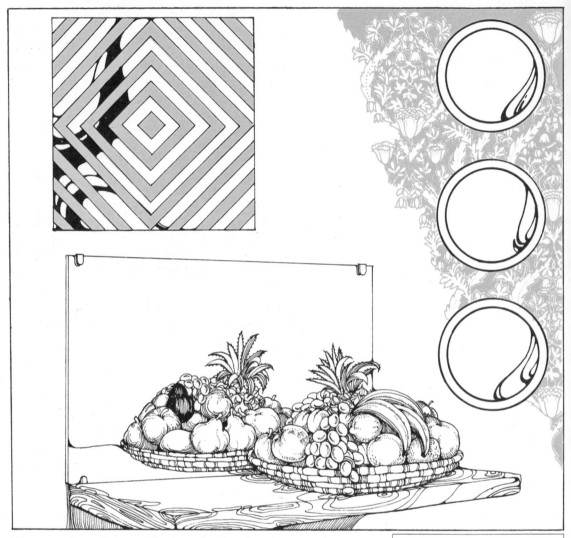

Mirrors reflect light and give depth, thereby creating the impression of spaciousness. This makes them ideal for small dark corners of a room, but beware of too much reflection in the wrong places. A mirror behind a chair for example is often disconcerting for people sitting opposite. Here are three unusual ways to use mirrors cleverly and practically.

Our first idea overcomes too much light being reflected from a large square mirror already on the wall. (Equally effective of course on any shaped large mirror.) With the help of masking tape an abstract design is painted on to the mirror so that unpainted spaces reflect a small amount of light in a pleasing way. The second idea positions three separate circular mirrors to create the impression of port windows in a small entrance hall. Here they reflect light without being too obvious. Place them on a side wall, half way between the front door and rear wall. In idea number three—a long mirror placed behind a small shelf proves extremely effective.

YOU WILL NEED:
For painted mirror:
Large square mirror
Roll of masking tape
Gloss or vinyl paint
For three mirrors
3 circular plastic
framed mirrors
3 1 in. No. 8 screws and
rawlplugs
For mirror over shelf:
3 ft. shelf
3×1 ft. mirror
3 brackets and screws
Rawlplugs

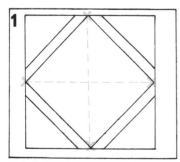

1 Painted mirrors: Mark centre point on each side. Stick masking tape across corner, (centre point on inside).

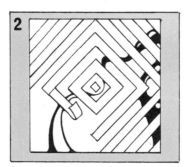

2 Leaving a tape's width between each row, stick strips out to corners then towards centre sticking tape in squares.

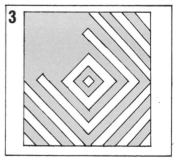

3 When the mirror is fully masked, paint it all over with gloss or vinyl paint. When it is quite dry remove the tape.

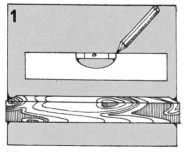

1 Mirror over shelf: with spirit level or straight timber batten draw pencil line on wall to mark shelf position.

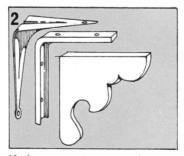

2 If the supports are to be seen use decorative brackets. For a low shelf use inexpensive angle brackets.

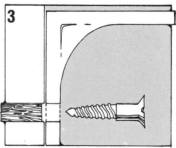

3 Drill and plug wall for supports. Screw in supports 6 in. from each end of shelf, and one in middle to prevent shelf from sagging.

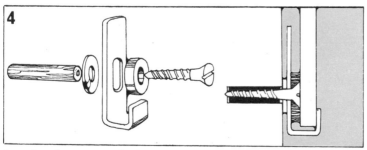

4 Attach mirror to wall above shelf, using corner clips. These are screwed into the wall as for the shelf supports.

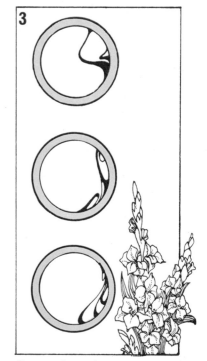

3 Repeat for other two mirrors positioning them so there is a 6 in. gap between each.

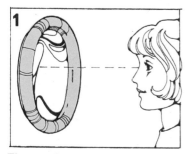

1 Three mirrors: position centre mirror at your eye level. Drill wall to take a $1\frac{1}{4}$ in. screw and place rawlplug in hole.

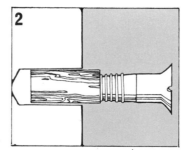

2 Screw the screw into hole, leaving just enough protruding to hook on mirror.

Boxes of Flowers

Plants are an essential part of homes and gardens, and although they look lovely grown on their own in pots, lots of plants together in a larger container make a really exciting display. Our free-standing boxes would look tremendous in an empty corner of a drawing room, or just as good standing outside the front door on a patio as seen above. And you can use the same method to make window boxes, which improve the appearance of any house. In case you are not naturally green-fingered, the pages overleaf are full of hints on growing plants for indoors and out.

YOU WILL NEED:
For free standing box:
2 pieces $\frac{3}{4}$ in. plywood, 12 in. square (for sides)
2 pieces $\frac{3}{4}$ in. plywood, 12 in. ×10$\frac{1}{2}$ in. (for sides)
1 piece $\frac{3}{4}$ in. plywood, 12 in. square (for base)
2 in. aluminium angle, 56 in. long
12 1 in. No. 8 round head aluminium screws
2 pieces $\frac{1}{2}$×2 in. pine 48 in. long
Woodworking adhesive
Nails · Drill
Hacksaw · hammer
sandpaper
For window box:
Materials as above—but measure window to gauge dimensions. Use birchwood plywood · Paint

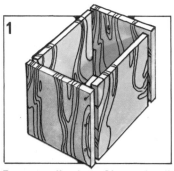

Free-standing box: Glue and nail plywood side-pieces together, shorter panels between longer ones.

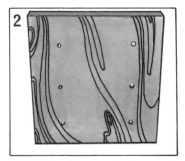

Drill 6 1 in. diameter holes evenly over plywood base for drainage.

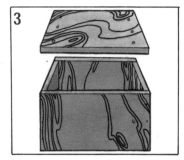

Glue and nail the base in place.

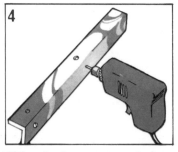

With a hacksaw cut angle into 4 14 in. lengths. Drill 2 3/16 in. holes in both sides of each piece 2 in. and 9 in. from one end.

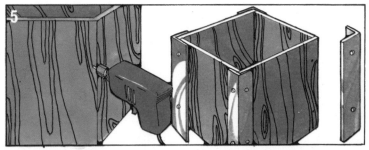

Drill 3/32 in. diameter pilot holes in sides of box. Then screw on angle, flush with top using screws specified opposite.

Cut the pine into 2 $10\frac{1}{2}$ in. and 2 $14\frac{1}{2}$ in. lengths.

Glue and nail to top of box. Round off corners of longer pieces with sandpaper after fitting.

Make a windowbox to fit your windowsill in the same way. Measure the sill to find dimensions for materials. Top of box should be 8–10 in. above sill. Use birchwood plywood; sand down.

Paint box with an undercoat, then finish off with a bright gloss paint.

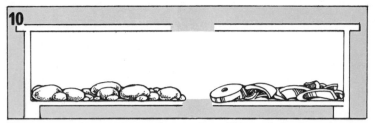

Plants grown in containers often perform disappointingly owing to a lack of air in the soil. To overcome this, place a layer of washed pebbles or pieces from broken flower pots or charcoal in the base of containers.

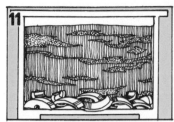

Fill up with potting compost, which is better than soil. Or else use a mixture of soil, leaf mould and fine silver sand.

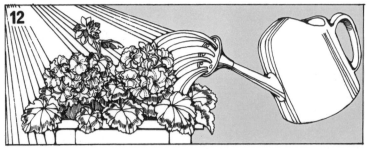

Disappointing results are also caused by lack of water. Where possible place the containers in semi-shade, and on very hot days, water your plants twice a day.

Use a proprietary plant food to replace the goodness in the soil. Administer as manufacturer's instructions.

Most shallow rooted bedding plants are suitable for container growing. Vary height and colours for interest.

Geraniums flower throughout the summer giving a continuous display of colour. They range in colour from white and soft pink through to deep crimson red.

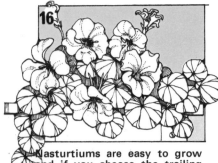

Nasturtiums are easy to grow and if you choose the trailing variety they will cascade down the sides of the box.

When transplanting from the garden or pots, water plants well beforehand and leave for an hour. Transplant in evening and retain as much soil on roots as possible. Water plants again as soon as they are re-planted.

Herbs grow well in windowboxes and give out a pleasant fragrance Parsley, fennel, chives, lemon balm and mint grow well, but grow mint in a flowerpot and place in the container otherwise it will swamp the others.

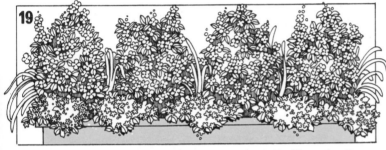

Plant spring bulbs in autumn. Choose crocus, daffodils and tulips to give consecutive bursts of colour. Plant wallflowers or forget-me-nots on top at the same time—they flower later and hide the dying leaves of the bulbs.

Two layers of daffodil bulbs give a great burst of colour. Bottom layer comes through to flower with top ones.

Hyacinths grow well in containers indoors or out and are available in various colours. Sink chrysanthemums grown in flower pots into the peat in your containers, so that they look as if they are growing freely.

Houseplants with variegated leaves such as ivy or coleus make attractive indoor displays. For indoor flowering plants, grow African Violets, Cyclamen, Poinsettia and Pelargonium.

Make our boxes any size and use them to cover unsightly man-hole covers or fit a particular corner.

Curtain Ideas

Here are a couple of simple, but novel curtain ideas. Cafe curtains are increasingly popular and understandably, as they look so fresh and informal. Make them in two or three layers to suit the size of your window and then open or close them at any height to let in as much or as little of the light, air and view that you want! They are super for kitchen and breakfast room windows, as well as for informal drawing or dining rooms.

An unusual way of softening the hard edges of a roller blind is simply draping a length of flimsy fabric around it. So so simple and yet the result is really pretty! Choose a patterned fabric to tone in with your blind if it is a plain colour, or alternatively if the blind has a design your drape should be plain.

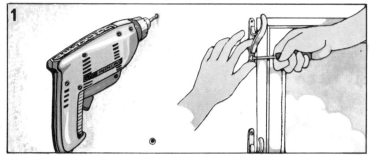

1 Cafe Curtains: Divide the height of your window into 3 and mount the rail at these intervals. To do this drill holes into the wall, plug with the rawlplugs and then screw in the supports.

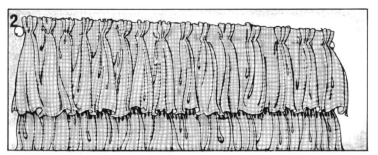

2 Cut strips of fabric to the finished depth of your curtains, plus 3 in. extra for hems. Curtains can either fall to the top of the pole below or, for complete seclusion and prevention of draughts, they can overhang.

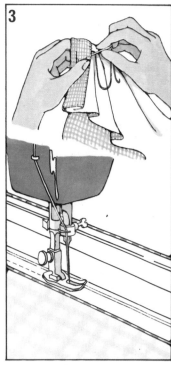

3 Turn double hems to wrong side on bottom and sides and stitch. Turn under single hem as top edge and machine stitch on pleated curtain tape.

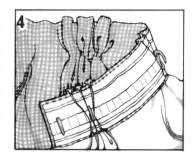

4 Draw up the cords so material falls into neat pleats. Insert curtain hooks and hang curtains.

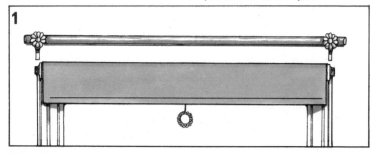

1 Blind Drapes: Mount a wooden curtain pole 3 in. above and lined up with window frame. Use decorative end stops as these will be on show. The poles can be in natural wood or have a painted finish to suit your colour scheme.

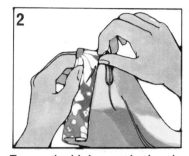

2 Turn up double hems at both ends of fabric and stitch (sides should be selvedge edges of fabric).

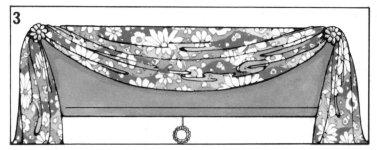

3 Drape the material over the end stops, so that it hangs evenly either side of the frame. If the window is wide catch the fabric up to the roller at the centre of the window.

More Curtain Ideas

Two more curtain ideas, and there can't be a window in your house that won't benefit from one of our ideas! We have even dealt here with those tricky sloping windows so often found nestling in sloping walls and ceilings. The Roman Blind, illustrated above right, provides an efficient and attractive answer. The pretty gingham pelmet with its sheer dreamy curtains would really look good anywhere. We chose gingham as it is so bright and fresh, but the ensemble would look just as fetching with any other fabric. Our instructions suggest using ready-made net curtains, but if this is now against your 'do-it-yourself' principles, just make up ordinary curtains using sheer material. (Instruction No. 4 in this project=R.S.=Right side of fabric.)

YOU WILL NEED for Roman Blind:

2 wooden curtain poles, slightly longer than *sides* of window	overlap window dimensions
	$\frac{1}{2}$ in. tape, 4 times length of window
$\frac{1}{2}$ in. and 1 in. timber battens, the width of the window	Small and large curtain rings
Fabric and lining to slightly	Several yards of strong nylon cord · Screws and rawlplugs

YOU WILL NEED
For Gingham Pelmet and Curtains:
Double and single curtain track to extend 6 in. either side of window
36 in. wide gingham, 4 times as long as curtain track, plus 6 in. extra to make tie-backs
Ready-made net curtains slightly longer than window
Coloured bauble trim, to match gingham
Curtain hooks and rings
Screw and rawlplugs
Wall hooks

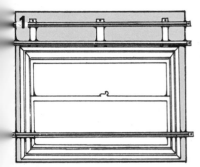

1 Gingham pelmets: Fix double rail curtain track 10 in. above window, and single track 14 in. above windowsill.

2 Cut and make up gingham into strips, 16 in. and 14 in. deep, both twice the width of the curtain track.

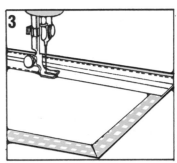

3 Turn up and stitch 1 in. hems along 1 long and both short sides. Turn under remaining edge and machine stitch on curtain tape.

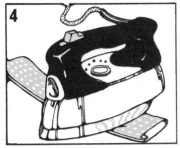

4 Cut two 12×6 in. gingham strips. R.S. inside fold each lengthwise. Stitch down long side. Turn to R.S. Press.

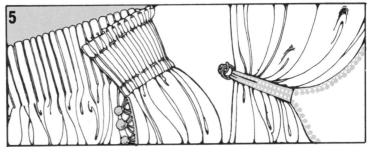

5 Sew curtain rings to either end of strips. Stitch trim of coloured baubles to net curtains and stitch curtain tape to top. Hang curtains and gingham strips. Screw hooks into wall 14 in. above sill. Hook back curtains.

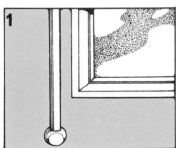

1 Roman Blind: Mount wooden curtain poles either side of window, extending slightly beyond top and bottom of frame.

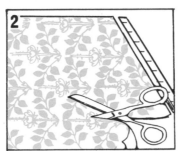

2 Cut fabric to fit between poles, allowing 2 in. hem either side and 8 in. extra on length. Place lining on back. Stitch side hems.

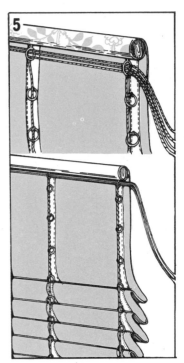

5 Thread cord through rings on blind as shown. Attach eyelets to top batten and continue cord through these.

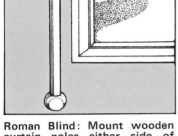

3 Machine 4 strips of ½ in. tape on wrong side. Sew curtain rings to sides of tape and blind every 3 to 4 in.

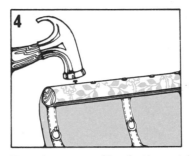

4 Turn hem over ½ in. batten at bottom and 1 in. batten at top. Secure with small tacks.

Going the Rounds

Nothing looks worse on a round table than a square tablecloth!
The sides hang raggedly and unevenly so that it just looks untidy
and un-tailored. The same goes for oval tables too—in fact what
round and oval tables need is round and oval tablecloths!
They are very easy to make, when you know just how, and if
they do take a little longer than their square counterparts, the
difference in appearance is so great, they are well worth the
slight extra trouble. Choose a washable, attractive fabric—easy
care sheeting is particularly recommended as it is sold in wide
widths—with an all-over pattern, (not one that goes just one
way). Trim round the edge with crisp matching lace to give a
pretty finishing touch.

YOU WILL NEED:
Fabric—see instruction
No. 1 and No. 9
for how to gauge amounts
Fancy trimming to go round
edge
Matching sewing thread

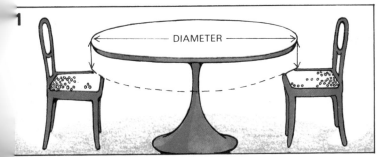

1 Measure diameter of table and add on the drop either side. On a dining table, the cloth should end approximately 10 to 12 in. from the top and clear chair seats by 2 in. On round occasional table, cloth should just touch the floor.

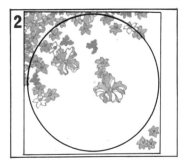

2 Use a square of material wide enough to cover table without seams, if possible. (See introduction.)

3 To cut a perfect circle—fold fabric in 4. Cut a piece of string approximately 3 ins. longer than required radius. Anchor other end to centre point with a pin. Draw an arc from one folded edge to the other and cut along this line.

5 Make trimming (see overleaf), or buy lace to fit round cloth edge. Hand or machine stitch all round cloth, close to hem.

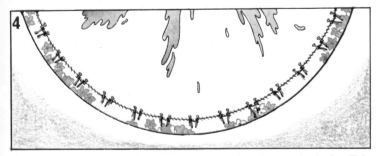

4 Turn up a double hem to the wrong side all round circle. Take up the fullness by making small pleats at frequent intervals. Secure these with pins. Hemstitch all round cloth.

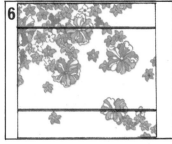

6 If fabric is too narrow, use full width for centre panel and join strips of appropriate size either side.

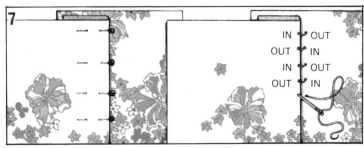

7 To match pattern fold on the right side. Press and pin. Sew small stitches bringing the needle in and out as shown. Note that the needle must be on the crease of the fabric itself for accuracy.

IN — OUT
OUT — IN
IN — OUT
OUT — IN

Turn to wrong side and machine stitch along this tacking line.

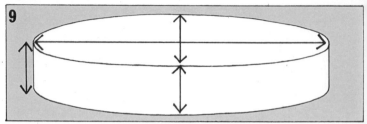

To make an oval tablecloth: measure width plus drop on either side of the table. Then measure the length and drop.

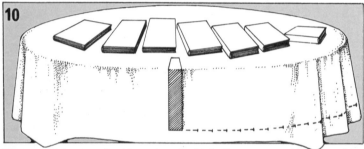

Cut material to required length and width. Open out and lay on table. Weight down with books. Bend a piece of card so that one part of it is length of drop, plus hem. Use this to mark the cutting line, place pins at regular intervals.

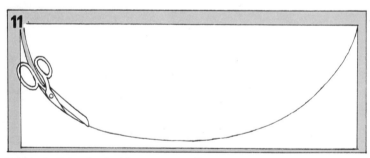

Fold in half to check sides are even. Cut out.

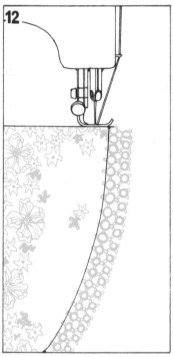

Hem bottom and trim as you did for circle.

The alternative to buying trimming which is often very expensive is to make your own. Maybe it does take a little longer, but it is very satisfying, and a sure way of getting exactly what you want!
YOU WILL NEED:
Tatting shuttle
Crochet thread

Use a shuttle not longer than $2\frac{3}{4}$ in. with a hook at the end. Wind crochet thread evenly round the shuttle, stopping short of the sides. Leave 15 in. length of thread.

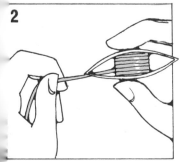

2 Hold shuttle between forefinger and thumb of right hand, and thread between forefinger and thumb of left hand.

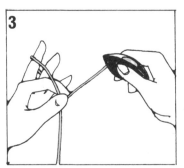

3 Bring thread round hand to form a large loop. Bend third and little finger to grip thread. Stretch centre finger to extend loop.

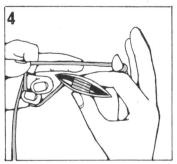

4 Catch thread with little finger of right hand. Thread should be tight, but not taut; practise if necessary.

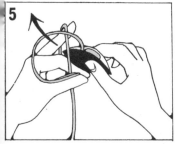

5 Swing thread from shuttle over left hand and thread shuttle through the loop this forms, from right to left.

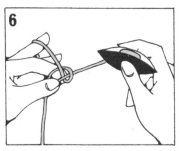

6 Jerk shuttle towards you to transfer loop as shown. (It is important to twist the loop on to the correct strand.)

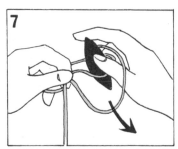

7 Swing thread to left to form a loop in the opposite direction to (5). Thread shuttle through from left to right.

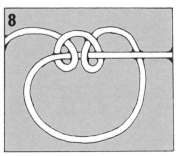

8 Jerk shuttle to transfer loop as before. This completes the double stitch used in tatting.

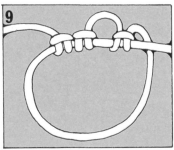

9 To form a 'picot' leave a $\frac{1}{4}$ in. space between first and second stitches so that it forms a loop when it is pushed up.

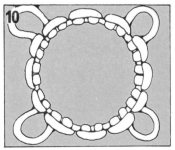

10 Work a ring with 4 picots each separated by 3 stitches. Complete by drawing shuttle thread tight so first and last stitches meet.

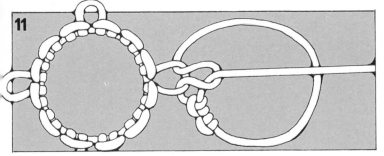

11 Work another ring the same as the first. Link this to the first by using the hook at the end of the shuttle to draw the thread through a picot in a loop and threading the shuttle through the loop.

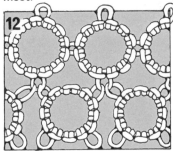

12 Work a double row of circles as shown, long enough to go right round the tablecloth. Sew it in place on cloth.

Beads are Beautiful

Anybody can make bead curtains—they are simple and easy and fun to make, yet they look extremely attractive and are very expensive to buy. They have lots of uses too. They can act as room dividers, separating the seating and eating parts of a lounge and dining room. Or smaller ones can be hung in an open doorway where they form a pretty visual screen whilst allowing the light and air through.

You can hang your strings of beads from a dowel which can then be suspended from cup hooks screwed into the door jamb or the ceiling. If it is specifically for a doorway, you could hang the strings from a curtain pole, the supports of which would be mounted over the doorway. When making the curtain, thread one complete string at a time to prevent tangling.

YOU WILL NEED:
1 ball of fine parcel string—natural colour
10 2 ft. lengths of garden cane
Small hacksaw
1 packet of rosewire (available from florists)
600 1½ in. lengths of ready cut cane
1 3 ft. curtain pole with supports or similar length of dowel and 2 cup hooks
Tissue paper

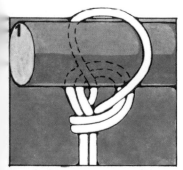

Saw the garden cane into 9 in. lengths. Cut a 14 ft. length of string and set on to curtain pole as shown.

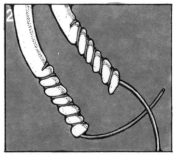

Bind bottom 2 in. of both ends of string with rosewire, separately, to make a stiff end for threading beads.

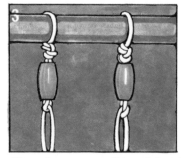

Thread on a small oval bead and knot the string to hold it tightly against the pole.

Knot the 2 lengths of string together about an inch from bead and thread on a round bead. Knot string again.

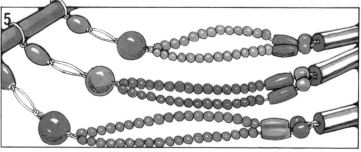

Thread about 12 in. with coloured beads, then thread on a 12 in. length of canes. Knot string before and after threading beads and canes in order to keep them in place.

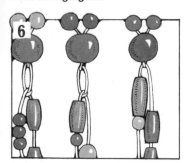

Thread alternate runs of beads and canes down string. Leave a short length of string between each group.

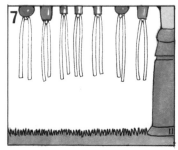

Stop threading 2–3 in. short of floor length—(for mounting over a doorway, curtain should be approximately 6 ft. 6 in. long).

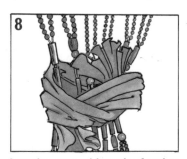

Attach a second length of string to pole. Thread similarly. Tie threads together with tissue paper as completed to prevent tangling.

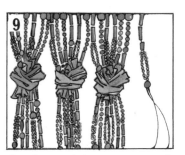

Continue right across pole, threading 30 lengths altogether. Tie strings together in bunches of six.

Mount pole supports over doorway (opposite side to opening side). Spread out strings across pole and hook on to supports.

Macrame Hanging Basket

Flowers in a pot suspended from the ceiling make a beautiful display and macrame is an ideal craft to use to make the 'cradle'. Macrame is a series of decorative knots—simple to do once you have got the hang of it—and can be used to make a multitude of things: hammocks, bags, belts and many, many more. The basket seen above will stretch to hold pots of any shape and most sizes, but don't hang up anything too big as the weight would be too great. You can suspend the basket from a hook, screwed securely into the ceiling. It will look particularly attractive hung near a window where the plant will also get all the air and light it needs. We suggest the kitchen as an ideal spot, where plants are always welcome, and this way, they won't clutter up the windowsill!

YOU WILL NEED:
42 yards of medium cotton twine, (parcel string is ideal)
2 brass or wooden rings, approx. 2 in. diameter
52 glass beads with large holes (choose a colour to tone with your pot)
Decorative pot approx. 3–7 in. high

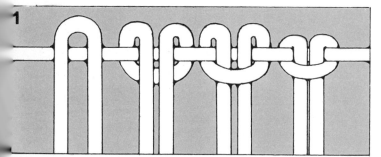

1 Cut 8 strands, each 5 yds. long. Bend double and attach to one of the rings with Lark's Heads, as shown.

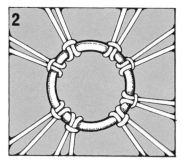

2 Position the strands in pairs around the ring as shown. This forms the base of the basket.

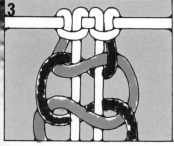

3 With 2 outside strands of one pair, form a square (flat) knot over two centre ones. Work each pair in this way.

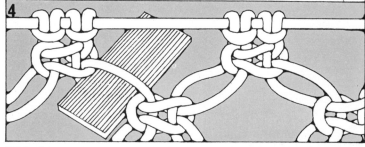

4 With 2 strands from one knot and 2 strands from next knot tie another square knot, 1 in. from the last. Use 1 in. wide stiff card between knots to space them. Repeat until you have 4 more knots.

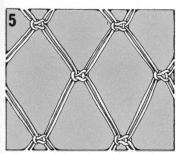

5 Work 4 more square knots as before, 2 in. from the previous row. Then work 4 more $2\frac{1}{2}$ in. away.

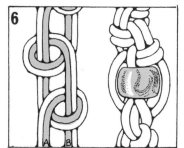

6 Work hanging cords with double chain knots, as shown. Thread beads on to strands A and B every $1\frac{1}{2}$ in. to 2 in., until cords measure 18 in.

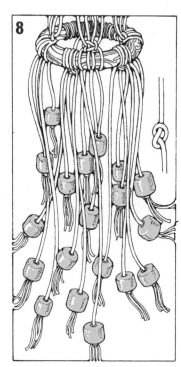

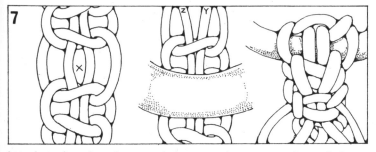

7 Attach to hanging ring—work 1 square knot on each cord. Leave small space, X, work 3 square knots. Place on ring, loop cord over pulling Z and Y through X. Work square knot with all 4 strands, on inside of ring. Thread a bead to each strand. Finish with overhand knot.

8 Cut 8 8 in. strands. Bend double, attach to bottom ring with Lark's Head and square knots. Thread on beads. Secure with overhand knots.

Kitchen Complement

A great idea for giving you that bit of extra storage capacity which every kitchen needs! Make this unit any size to fit that awkward little space that you have been wondering what to do with. If you have a larger area, make two units, as we have done, and bank them up together. Use them for food storage, pots and pans, utensils or what you will. (We have shown our units completely covered with patterned tiles. See instructions 9, 10 and 11 for alternative suggestions.)

Our cannisters are real money savers! Jars are emptied every week in ordinary kitchen use and so often, just thrown away. Keep them instead and make yourself a whole range of cannisters to hold flour and sugar and tea and coffee beans and dried fruit and ... the list is endless! Have a look at the cost of cannisters in the shops, just to see how much money you are saving! Tins perhaps are not in such constant use these days, and yet are invaluable for biscuits and cakes. You will probably find you can buy them from your local sweet shop for no more than a few pence.

YOU WILL NEED:
For the shelving unit
½ in. thick plywood or laminated chipboard (see opposite for sizes or buy according to the size unit you require)
1 in. square battens—16 ft. long
Woodworking adhesive
4 dozen ¾ in. panel pins
Wood stain or primer, undercoat and gloss paint
Tiles (optional)

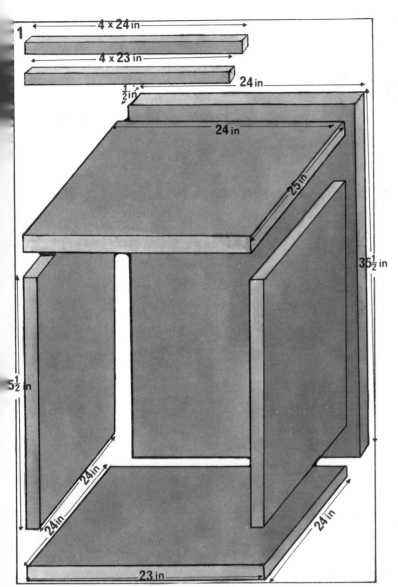

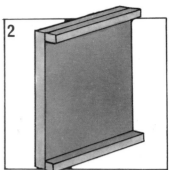

Using adhesive, stick 24 in. long battens flush with the top and bottom of the side panels.

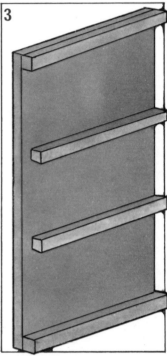

Cut the board to the sizes shown above, using a panel saw. Measurements for the 2 inside shelves are the same as those for the unit's base. In addition, saw the 1 in. thick batten into 4 lengths 24 in. long and 4 lengths 23 in. long.

Using adhesive, stick 23 in. battens, 1 in. in from the front and flush with back of side panels, at 10½ in. intervals.

Tap in 3 panel pins to each batten for added strength.

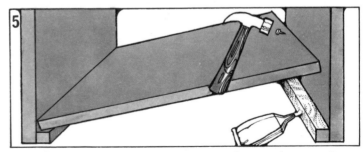

Slide in base of unit, resting it on two bottom battens. Secure with adhesive and panel pins.

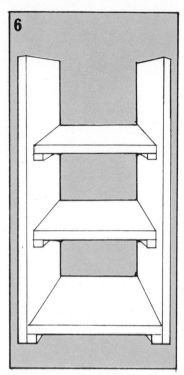

6 Insert remaining shelves, securing them in the same way with adhesive and panel pins.

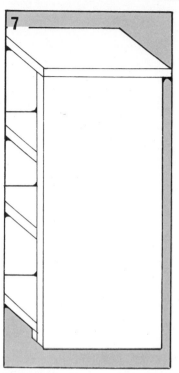

7 Glue top in place so it is flush with the front (there is a 1 in. overhang at the back). Secure with panel pins.

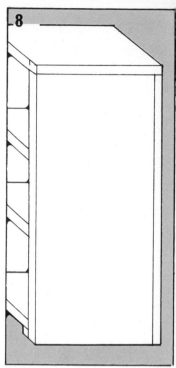

8 Glue on the back panel, securing it with panel pins. It fits under the top overhang to give a neat finish.

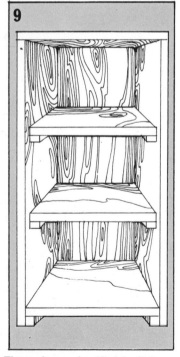

9 The unit can be 'finished' in a number of ways. Stain with coloured varnish so woodgrain shows through.

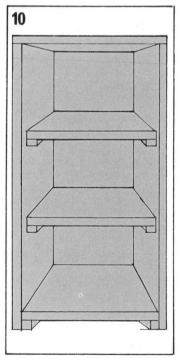

10 *Or* prime wood, then paint with 2 undercoats and finish with a gloss paint to give a hardwearing finish.

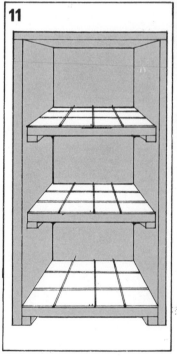

11 *Or* paint or stain unit, except for top of shelves. Glue tiles to inside shelves. (Follow manufacturer's instructions.)

Wash tins and jars thoroughly in soapy water and leave to dry.

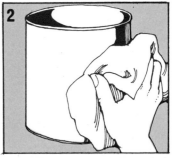

Rub the outsides with a cloth moistened with methylated spirit. Make sure none goes inside or round edges of container.

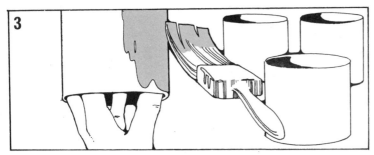

Paint tins and jars, first with primer, then undercoat and finally gloss paint. Leave some jars unpainted.

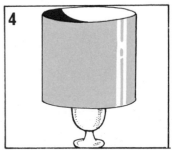

Rest the painted jars on egg cups, or similar objects smaller than the base of the jar to give a neatly finished rim.

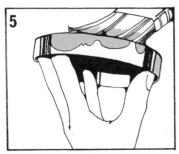

Paint the outside of all lids in the same way, making sure no paint comes into contact with the rim or the inside.

Cut sticky labels into strips, suitably sized to fit the jars. Using Letraset, letter on the names of intended contents.

If you like draw decorative borders round the edges of labels. Stick to jars and tins.

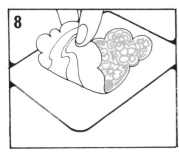

Alternatively, cut out decorative motifs from 'peel-and-stick' plastic covering (sold to cover work-tops).

Or use the plastic as a stencil to paint a pattern or name in a contrasting shade. Cut out shapes from plastic, stick to painted jar. Then paint jar in another shade. When dry, peel off plastic, so pattern stands out in a different colour.

Wooden Symphony

Windchimes gently swaying by an open window make the most beautiful sound, somehow reminiscent of far-off gentle Oriental music. The sound it makes will vary according to the materials you use; we recommend wood and cane which gives a pleasant reedy sound, rather than metal which tends to be harsher and more resonant. Scope for making windchimes is endless and the rules are simple. Work and complete one string at a time so as not to end up with an inextricable tangle, and whether working on a circle or a straight piece of cane, make sure the balance is right so it hangs correctly. Copy our simple, pretty set, or design your own. Either way it is no more than an evening's work, which is not bad for the years of pleasure it will provide.

YOU WILL NEED:
6 in. cane handbag handle, or 8 in. wooden ring
Beads, 1½ in. length of bamboo, wooden shapes, brass bells
Polyurethane to stain the wood, in blue and red
Strong linen thread—
8 lengths approximately 18 in. long
4 lengths approximately 9 in. long
2 lengths approximately 20 in. long to suspend mobile.

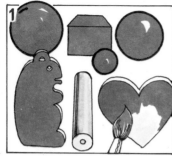

1 Stain beads and wooden shapes with polyurethane—half in red, half in blue. Leave bamboo lengths and cane ring natural.

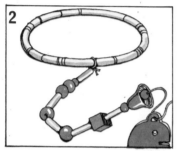

2 Tie an 18 in. strand to ring. Thread beads on at random interspersed with cane. Finish with a wooden shape.

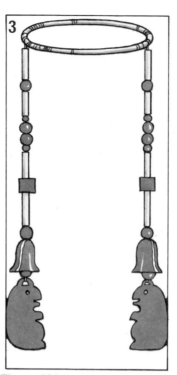

3 Tie an 18 in. strand to ring exactly opposite and thread with the same combination of beads, bamboo and wooden shapes.

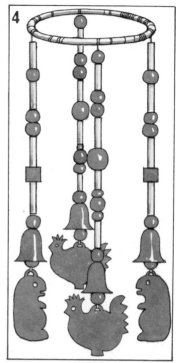

4 Tie on 2 more 18 in. strands opposite each other in between first 2. Thread in different combination, ending with wooden shapes.

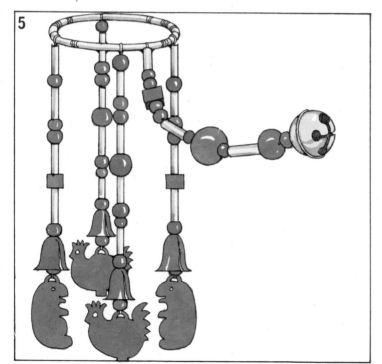

5 Tie remaining 18 in. strands between first four. Thread each with beads and bamboo ending with a bell. Finish threading each strand before starting another. Tie strands together in pairs to avoid tangling.

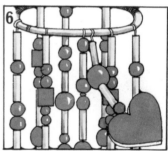

6 Tie the 4 short threads between each pair of long threads. Thread with beads and bamboo ending with a shape.

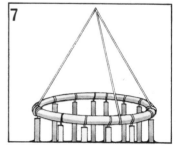

7 Spread threads out evenly around ring. Tie 2 threads to top of ring either side to hang it by.

Cork Pin Board

Proof that a kitchen pin board need not be an eyesore—here's one that would look good on any wall and will give a kitchen new status. Use it for shopping lists, bills, or even small bunches of herbs. It could not be easier to make and yet it could hardly be more effective. You could of course, use it anywhere in the house—in a bedroom for example to hang up beads and bangles. Just right for a teenager's 'pad'!

Old frames are easy to find, in junk shops or tucked away in the corners of attics and store rooms. Don't throw them away, even if they look old and scratched and ugly. A quick clean-up, and a lick of paint and you will be surprised at the difference.

YOU WILL NEED:
Old frame
Dark brown cork tiles
Hardboard
Impact glue
Small nails
Round-eyed picture screws
Wire or strong thread
Sharp craft knife · hammer
Paint

1 Remove backing and clean frame if necessary. If it is plain wood, strip, polish or stain it, or paint it to match your colour scheme. If it is gold, touch up with gold paint if required.

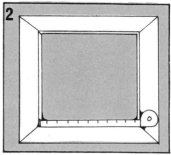

2 Measure width and depth of frame at back. Cut piece of hardboard to fit these measurements.

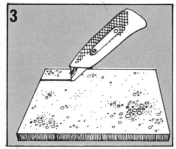

3 Using a sharp knife cut cork tiles to fit hardboard exactly.

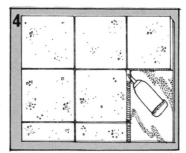

4 Glue cork to hardboard. Smear glue on edge of cork at joins so they fit together tightly.

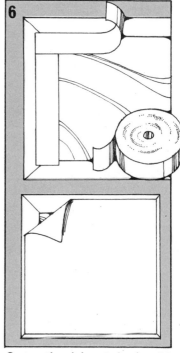

6 Cover the join at back with masking tape, or glue brown paper right over the back of frame.

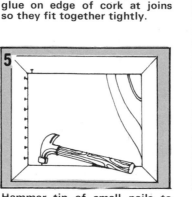

5 Hammer tip of small nails to inside edge at back of frame. Put cork and hardboard in frame. Hammer nail tops across hardboard to keep it in place.

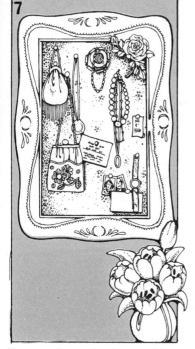

7 You can hang the frame either vertically . . . .

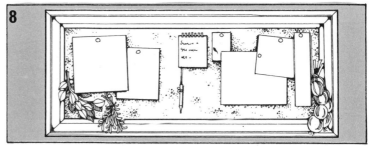

8 . . . or horizontally to suit the space available. Screw hooks to the back of frame and hang up using wire or strong thread.

Ideas for Beds

Bring the romance of the olde worlde back a little by turning your bed into a 4-poster. It's easily done and fun, too! The original reason for heavily draped beds was to keep out the draughts that howled unchecked round those huge castle rooms. So in order not to practically suffocate within the majesty of your 4-poster, choose flimsy, sheer fabric. It will look pretty without being too heavy and overbearing for today's smaller rooms.

The other idea shown here is ideal for prettying-up a single bed (although it would be just as effective on a double). Floaty fabric is simply draped over curtain poles mounted on the ceiling.

For both these ideas, and the ones on the next page, the curtain track should be secured to a joist in the ceiling or else it will not be firm enough. This may mean changing the position of your bed! Tap the ceiling to locate the joists—the sound will be less hollow over them.

YOU WILL NEED
For 4-poster:
Double curtain track, twice length of bed, and width plus 12 in.
Curtain fabric—for valance— $1\frac{1}{2}$ **times length of track and 12 ins. deep · Drill · screws**
For curtain round bed—see instructions Nos. 3 and 4. Length should be ceiling to floor plus 6 ins. for hems
Curtain tape to fit all curtains and valance
Curtain hooks and rings
Matching synthetic thread
For curtain pole idea:
2 curtain poles with decorative endstops, slightly longer than width of bed
Curtain fabric
Matching synthetic thread and trim · Drill · screws

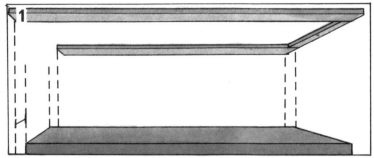

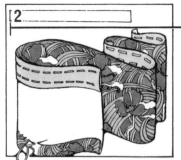

4-Poster: Gently tap ceiling to locate joists. Screw double curtain track to ceiling, parallel with bed sides, but 6 in. to 1 ft. wider (depending on joists). Screw length of track in line with foot of bed to link the side pieces.

Cut and join fabric for valance, (see You Will Need). Hem 1 long edge. Turn in edge of other. Stitch on curtain tape.

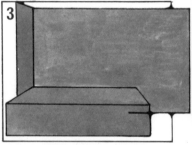

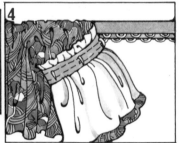

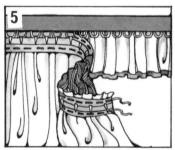

If curtains are to be drawn round bed, make 2, each 1½ times length along sides of bed and halfway across end.

Or make 4 curtains, each from single width of fabric to fit at each corner. Pull up tape on valance and hook to outer track.

Hem edges and bottom of curtains. Turn in top edge and stitch on tape. Pull up tape. Insert hooks. Hook curtains to inner track.

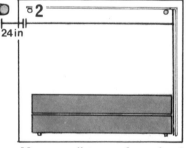

Curtain pole drapes: Tap ceiling to locate joists. Screw in curtain poles supports for 2 poles slightly wider than bed, one pole should be approx. 4 in. away from wall and the other parallel with end of bed (depending slightly on joist). Hook on poles and screw on end stop.

Measure distance from headboard or floor skirting board, up to ceiling and along to second pole. Add on 24 in.

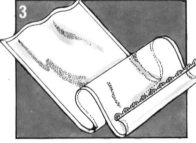

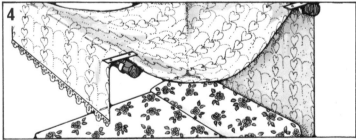

Make up material to this length, slightly wider than bed. Hem one short edge and both long edges. Stitch on trimming to other short edge.

Secure untrimmed short edge behind headboard or tack to skirting board. Drape material over curtain poles allowing a 12 in. drop over foot of bed. (Excess material should drape softly in between poles.)

More Ideas for Beds

Two more ideas to give you the prettiest beds in the neighbourhood! For those that felt our 4-poster idea was just a little too much of a good thing, try our canopy idea. It's less majestic perhaps, but rather less ambitious too, and will make your bedroom just as distinctive. (In instructions for this project —No. 3 = R.S. = right sides of fabric.) And finally an extremely pretty idea, just the thing for an ultra-feminine little miss's room. The effect is achieved by 2 curtains flowing out from a single pole, mounted along the ceiling directly over the middle of the bed.

Make sure all ceiling fixtures are screwed through to joists.

YOU WILL NEED for the single bed idea:

3 ft. curtain pole with decorative end stops	times length of pole)
Wooden rings and curtain hooks	Pencil pleat curtain tape
	Matching synthetic thread
Sheer fabric (for 2 curtains, width of each equals 1½	Decorative towel rings
	Drill · Screws

YOU WILL NEED
For the canopy idea:
2 timber battens, 1 × 2 in., the width of the bed plus 12 in.
2 timber battens, 1 × 2 × 18 in.
Curtain fabric for canopy—
2 strips, 12 in. deep, 6 in. wider than long battens
'Iron-on' stiffening, for canopy
Brass-headed studs
Curtain fabric for back curtain—1½ times width of bed, floor to ceiling length, plus 3 in.
Curtain fabric for side curtains—(2) 48 in. wide, floor to ceiling length plus 3 in.
¾ yd. fabric for ties
Curtain tape to fit curtains
Drill · Screws

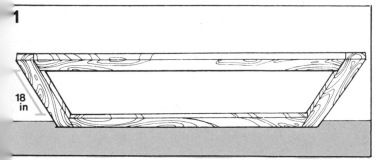

1

18 in

Canopy idea: Locate ceiling joists and screw on long timber battens, 1 at wall (at head of bed), the other parallel 18 in. away (on ceiling). Screw on 2 short battens at right angles to these extending back to wall.

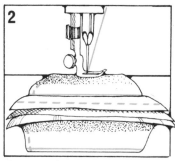

2

Cut canopy fabric (see You Will Need). Iron stiffening to wrong side of 1 piece. R.S. together stitch round 3 sides of strips.

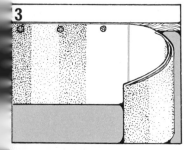

3

Turn to right side. Turn over top edge and tack to batten, (furthest away from wall) using decorative studs.

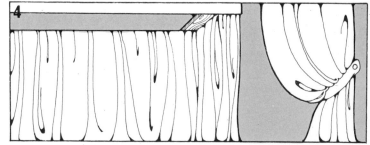

4

Make up back curtain (see You Will Need). Hem sides and 1 end. Sew on curtain tape, pull up. Tack to wall batten. Make side curtains. Hem sides and 1 end. Stitch on curtain tape, pull up. Tack to side battens. Make side ties, tack to wall. Slot curtain through.

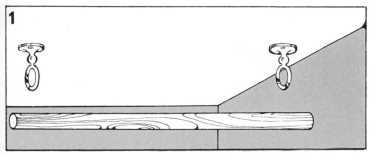

1

Single pole: Double curtains: Locate joist in ceiling. Drill and screw in pole supports at right angles to wall. Use pole to measure distance between supports and allow room for decorative end stops.

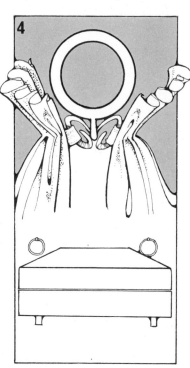

4

Hook curtain on to wooden rings. Screw decorative towel rings to wall, 6 in. either side of bed and thread curtains through.

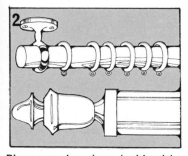

2

Place wooden rings (sold with pole) on pole and hook on to supports. Screw on end stops.

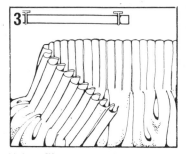

3

Using flimsy material make up 2 curtains, 1½ times length of pole. Hem edges and stitch curtain tape to top.

New Life for Bed Linen

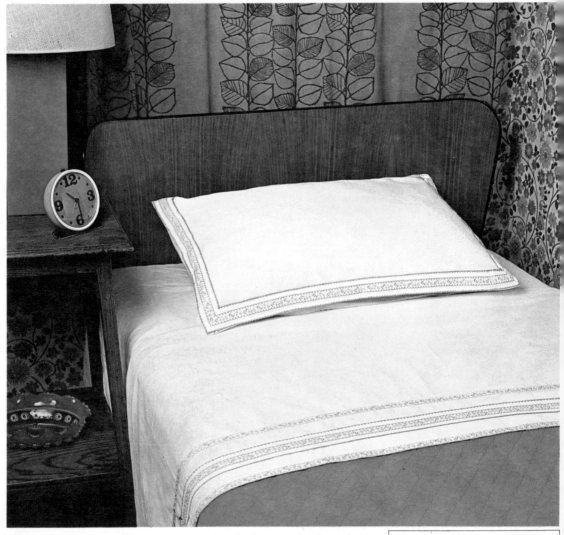

When sheets and pillowcases are beginning to look rather tired and old, but still have lots of wear in them, liven them up with some gay trimmings. (Remember to make sure you only use washable trimmings however.) Lengthen short sheets, too, by attaching a strip of bright coloured fabric and then make pillowcases from the same fabric to team up. A clever way to overcome a problem!

We give instructions for making your own sheets and pillowcases, which nowadays means economic sense; and also means you can select the colour and pattern you really like. Try it sometime!

YOU WILL NEED:
For 1 Single Sheet:
3 yds. × 70 ins. sheeting (sheeting is usually sold in standard bed widths)
For 1 Pillowcase:
$\frac{2}{3}$ yd. × 70 in. sheeting
Trimming for Sheet and Pillowcase:
$2\frac{2}{3}$ yd. braid, $2\frac{1}{2}$ in. wide
4 yds. braid 1 in. wide
Matching sewing thread
(These amounts will vary according to how you apply the trimming. Measure your sheet and buy trimming accordingly)

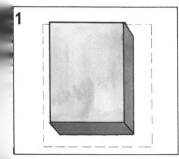

1 To make a sheet, measure length and width of bed, plus depth of mattress. Add 12 in. extra on all 4 sides.

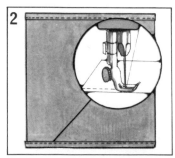

2 Turn ½ in. hems to the wrong side at ends of sheet, and stitch. Repeat along sides (if not selvedge edges).

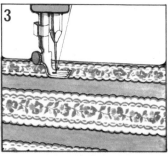

3 Select braiding to tone with the sheet. Machine stitch it in rows on the right side of the top of the sheet.

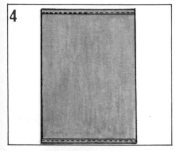

4 *For a pillowcase:* cut a piece of sheeting 62×20 in. Turn ½ in. hems to wrong side at each end and stitch in place.

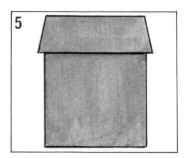

5 With right sides inside, turn up 2 in. Turn the single piece down over this.

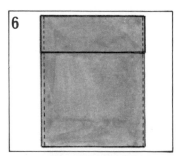

6 Stitch the side edges to form a bag. Stitching should be ½ in. from the edge.

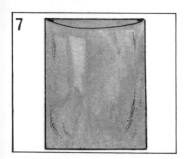

7 Reach inside the flap and turn the pillowcase inside out.

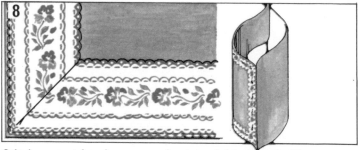

8 Stitch same trimming as on sheet to right side of pillowcase, on side with the flap inside. Mitre corners of trim and machine as close as possible to edge. Separate fabric when machining inner edge and stitch to topside only.

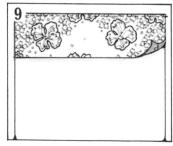

9 To lengthen a short sheet, un-pick top hem and, right sides together, stitch on 18 in. deep strip of contrasting colour fabric.

10 Hem edge to wrong side. When sheet is placed on bed—right side down—the right side of the contrasting piece will be turned over the blankets. Make a pillowcase as described but use the same material as the contrasting sheet trim.

Bedroom Luxury

For sheer unashamed luxury, make this fur bedspread for your bed. It simply oozes a feeling of cosiness and gracious living. Our instructions are for a box-shape bedspread which keeps the fur clear of the castors and so unmarked. It also has a neat, tailored look, which is important in a small bedroom. As you make the bedspread, avoid pressing the fur, which will flatten the pile. It is advisable to have synthetic fur fabric dry-cleaned which you may be able to do in a coin-operated machine. Check first, though, as some are too hot for synthetic materials.

YOU WILL NEED:
6 yds. of 54 in. wide synthetic fur fabric
Matching synthetic thread
$1\frac{1}{2}$ in. long dressmaker's pins
$\frac{1}{2}$ in. tape for edging

Cut a length of fur 9 ft. long for centre panel. Test on bed for length—it should reach base at end plus 2 in.

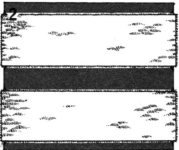

Cut 2 strips 7 ft. × 2 ft. 3 in. for side panels. (Measurements allow for seam and hem turnings.)

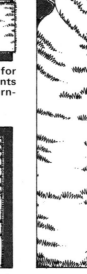

Right sides together, place short edge of one side panel at right angles across bottom end of centre panel. Pin, with pins placed horizontally so machining can be done over them. This prevents one side stretching more than the other.

Ease side panel round corner and pin long edges of centre and side panels together. Repeat process with other side panel.

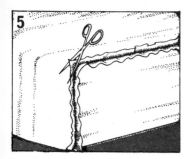

Put bedspread, pile side down on bed and adjust corners on wrong side to fit exactly. Trim off point on corner of side panel.

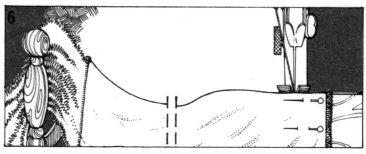

Using a long machine stitch and synthetic thread, stitch approximately ¾ in. in from edge. Make sure bulk of fur is on left hand side of machine as you sew. Support it on a chair to prevent weight pulling on stitching.

Turn to right side and gently comb out any trapped fur along the seam line.

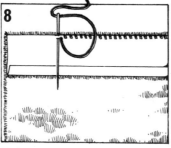

To hem, sew tape along all edges with close oversewing stitches. This prevents the fur wearing away at the edge.

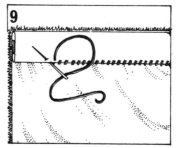

Turn tape to wrong side and hem down edge using small hemming stitches.

Bath and Basin Mats

Whatever floor covering you have in your bathroom, mats by the bath and basin are really essential—ready to catch water spills and drips, talcum powder and so on. They are easy and quick to make. Use towelling which can be put into the washing machine with the weekly wash and choose colours that match and blend with your general colour scheme. Make them dramatic by putting on a large motif in the middle in a strikingly contrasting colour, and use left-over bits of towelling to make matching face flannels.

YOU WILL NEED:
for basin mat
Towelling 20×30 in.
Towelling in contrasting colour 12×12 in.
Matching synthetic thread
Piece of thin wire

for bath mat
Towelling 36×40 in.
Towelling in contrasting colour 12×12 in.
Matching synthetic thread
½ in. thick foam 35×18 in.

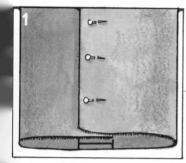

Basin mat: Right side inside, fold 20×30 in. towelling, bringing sides to middle. Overlap edges by 2 in. and pin.

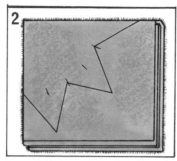

Draw and cut out a star-shaped patch from contrasting colour towelling.

Position star on top of mat (i.e. side with no seam), towards one end. Pin in place through single fabric only.

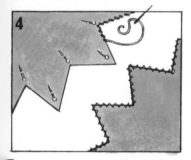

Turn mat over, remove pins from seam. Open out fabric. Oversew star in place or machine using zig-zag stitch.

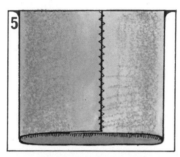

With star inside fold fabric side to middle again, overlapping edges. Machine with zig zag stitch along one raw edge.

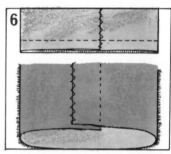

Turn mat right way out and machine along second raw edge. (This gives a flat seam.) Turn wrong side out. Stitch along lower edge.

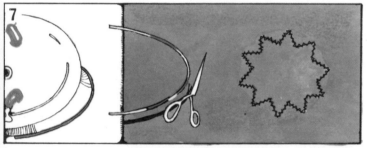

Bend wire round base of basin pedestal to get the exact shape. Place wire on mat, above star-shape and cut out ½ in. lower than wire (i.e. towards star).

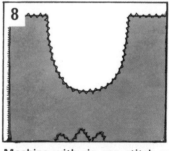

Machine with zig zag stitch or oversew round the raw edges of the cut out shape and the ends to complete mat.

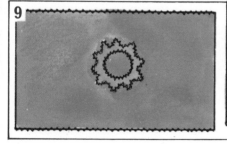

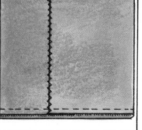

Bath mat; cut towelling in the same way and sew on star. (We added a circle also.) Machine zig zag stitch or oversew down both long centre edges (singly) to stop fraying. Fold as before and machine along short ends. Turn mat right side out.

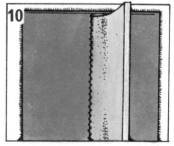

Cut ½ in. thick foam to same size and insert it in mat. Leave centre seam open so foam can be removed for washing.

Bathroom-Three-In-One

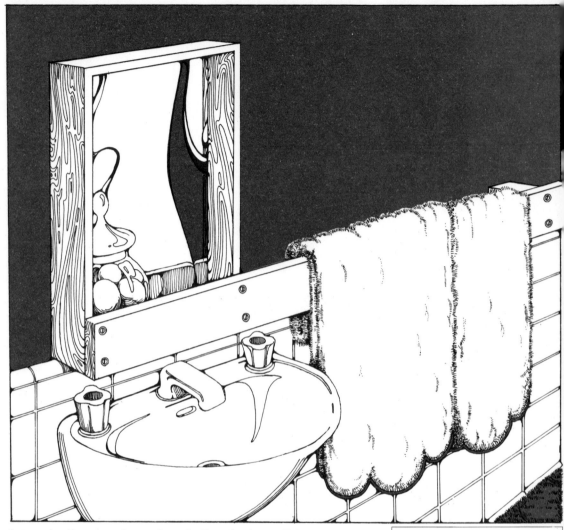

A towel rail, cosmetic storing shelf and mirror all in one super 'chunky' unit. Wood will merge easily into any bathroom decor, enhancing it with its own natural character. It should be well coated with clear polyurethene to protect it from watery splashes. The shelf is incorporated into the mirror frame and is ideal for cosmetic bottles and shaving tackle. Adjust the length of the towel rail to suit the space available in your bathroom.

YOU WILL NEED:
Plywood $\frac{1}{2} \times 24 \times 18$ in.
Woodworking adhesive
Contact adhesive
Nails
Spirit level · Drill
Mirror 24×18 in.
Pine (for frame) 3×1×90 in.
Pine (for shelf) 4×1×54 in.
Wood block 3×3×1$\frac{1}{2}$ in.
Cream coloured wood stopper
4 2 in. No. 8 woodscrews
2 1$\frac{1}{4}$ in. No. 8 woodscrews
4 2$\frac{1}{2}$ in. No. 8 woodscrews
6 2 in. brass woodscrews and countersunk cups
Clear polyurethane varnish

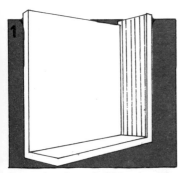

1 Saw pine into 2 25 in. lengths and 2 18 in. lengths. Nail to form a frame round plywood panel. Cover nail heads with cream coloured wood stopper.

2 Drill 3/16 in. diameter hole at each corner of panel. Countersink holes so that head of screw will be flush with the wood.

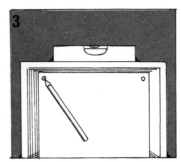

3 Level frame in place on wall, using the spirit level. Mark screw holes with a pencil.

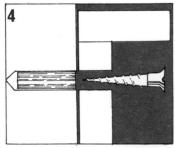

4 Drill $1\frac{1}{2}$ in. into wall. Push in rawlplugs and screw panel to wall using 2 in. No. 8 woodscrews.

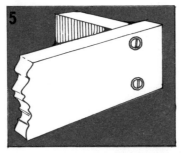

5 1 in. from end of pine shelf, screw on a $3 \times 3 \times 1\frac{1}{2}$ in. wood block using $1\frac{1}{4}$ in. No. 8 woodscrews.

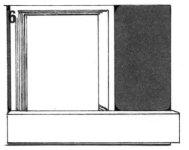

6 Get someone to hold the rail so it fits flush with the side and bottom of the mirror.

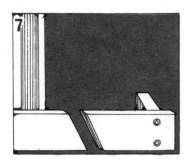

7 With this in position, mark round the block on shelf with a pencil. Use a spirit level to make sure it's level.

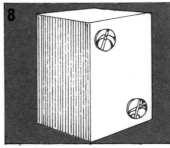

8 Unscrew block and saw it in half. Fix one half to the wall using rawlplugs and $2\frac{1}{2}$ in. No. 8 woodscrews.

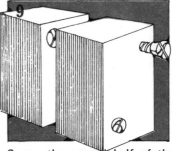

9 Screw the second half of the block to the first bit, avoiding the first set of screw holes.

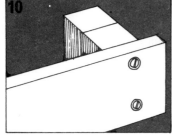

10 Screw rail to block using brass screws set in brass countersunk cups to give a decorative finish.

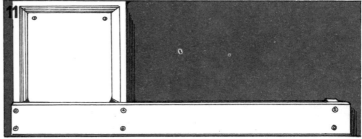

11 Screw other end of plank to each side of mirror frame in same way. Coat wood with clear polyurethane for protective finish. Fix mirror in place with screws provided, or use a mirror tile bonded with contact adhesive.

Grecian Trim

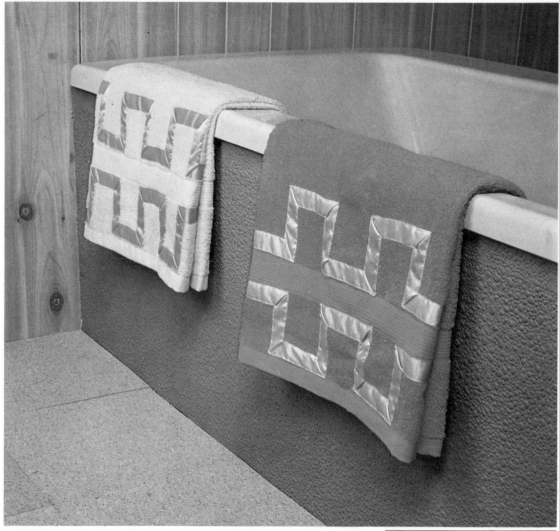

A touch of luxury for your bathroom,—Greek-key trims for towels. Although there is no need to add decorative trims to towels, it does seem to give a little extra distinction and tends to take away the starkness from strong plain colours. When you buy the ribbon trim, do make sure it is washable, and even better that it has the same 'washcode' as your towels. Choose contrasting colours or if you have two colours of towel, do as we have done, by trimming each of them in the colour of the other.

YOU WILL NEED:
For each towel
Approx. 6 yds. of washable ribbon trim
Matching synthetic thread

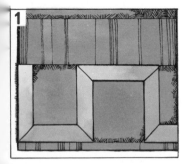

1 Work trim row between bound end and pile-less strip first. Adjust size of pattern if necessary.

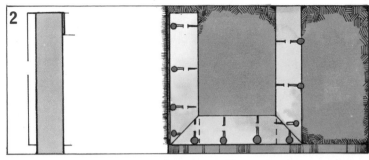

2 Turn under $\frac{1}{2}$ in. at end of ribbon. Pin $3\frac{1}{4}$ in. of ribbon at edge of towel parallel with long side. Mitre and pin corner in direction shown and pin $3\frac{1}{4}$ in. along towel parallel with short side. Mitre and pin corner in direction shown.

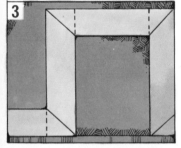

3 Pin $3\frac{1}{4}$ in. ribbon back up towel, parallel with first line. Mitre corner and repeat with next $3\frac{1}{4}$ in. across towel. Mitre as shown.

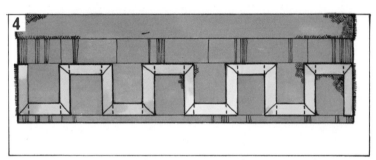

4 Continue in this way, pinning pattern across towel, making sure you mitre each corner in same direction as first 4. This ensures the correct width of the pattern each time.

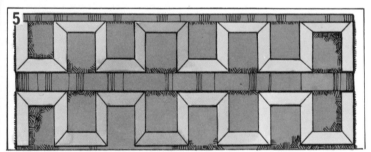

5 Turn towel round to pin second row back across towel. This makes it easier to pin mitred corners in correct direction. Both rows should be pinned in place before machining, to allow for minor adjustments to be made if necessary.

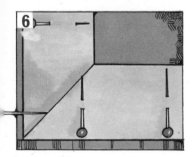

6 Remove underlying pins before machining. The mitred corners will be held in place by the second pin.

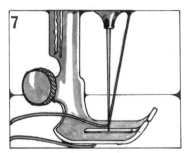

7 Thread up machine with braid colour on top and towel colour in bobbin to avoid unsightly stitching on towel back.

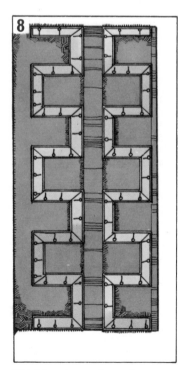

8 Machine over pins where possible. If braid puckers, pull towel taut to take up surplus. (Repinning means adjusting whole row.)

Towelling Curtains

Towels make good bathroom curtains. The texture, of course, is at home in such a setting and the material absorbs steam and moisture without looking limp and tired. Match curtains to towels for a co-ordinated look, or trim them both with matching braid.

YOU WILL NEED:
Towelling—1½ times width of window and slightly longer than top to sill
(You can use ordinary bathroom towels joined together)
Washable braid—(amount will depend on width of curtains and number of trimming rows)
Matching synthetic thread
1 in. wide curtain tape—same width as curtain

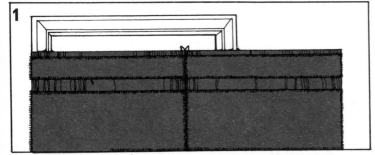

1 Cut towelling so it measures 1½ times the width of the window and frame. If using bathroom towels, join 2 together if necessary. The curtain should be long enough to cover the sill.

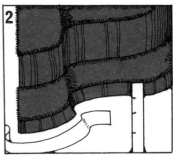

2 Measure depth of bound ends of towel and use braid of the same width. (It is usually 1 in. deep.)

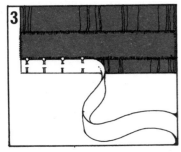

3 Pin braid along bound end, as close to edge as possible.

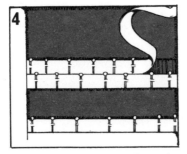

4 Pile-less strip is usually twice the measurement of bound end. Pin 2 rows of braid close together over it.

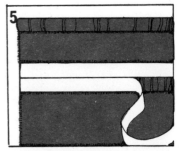

5 Pin braid to pile-less strip at other end of towel if liked. Do not trim bound edge at the end.

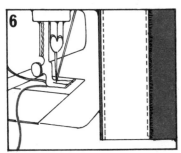

6 Thread up machine with braid colour on top and towel in bobbin. Machine braid to curtain at very edge.

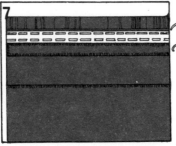

7 Pin 1 in. wide curtain tape to back of towel just below braid-free bound end. Machine in place.

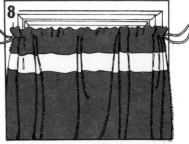

8 Draw up tape a little to make heading stand upright. Adjust cords to suit width of window.

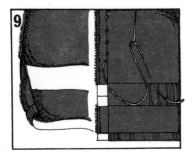

9 Hang curtain. If towel curls outwards when hung, turn in side edges and hem by hand.

10 Machine rows of braid to bathroom towels in the same way to match curtains. (Trim both bound ends in this case.)

You're an Artist

Add a completely new dimension to the rooms in your house by painting a mural on the walls. You don't need to be very clever at drawing or painting to achieve super results. You could for example with the use of masking tape, create an exciting, eye-catching geometric design in a drawing room, which you'd soon find was a great talking point! Our lovely landscape idea above would be super for a child's playroom or nursery, and provides an ideal setting for children's 'fantasy-land' games. Our graph pattern is approximately 1 square to 10 ins. but if necessary you could adapt this easily to suit the space you have available. Simply divide the wall space you have by the number of squares on our pattern and draw the pattern up accordingly.

YOU WILL NEED:
Soft pencil
Long rule or plumb line
Paint brush and painting pads
Vinyl or emulsion paints
String

Measure the two walls you are going to paint (pattern can be centred or not, according to room). Divide walls into 10 in. squares using rule or plumb line. Transfer above pattern to graph paper. Draw up to fit on walls, and transfer outlines to wall areas. Use pencil tied to a length of string as compasses for sun, rainbow and hills outline.

Begin with lighter colours, so errors can be covered up with subsequent colours.

Outline each part before painting it. Load small brush well with paint and use long sweeping strokes.

Fill in large areas with wide bristle brush, or, even better, paint pads, which give a neat outline.

Watch that Panda

Another mural idea for a child's room and this one perhaps needs even less artistic merit. This idea looks particularly good if the Panda is drawn on the door. Paint the lower half of the wall and door in one colour and the upper part in a contrasting colour so that the friendly Panda looks as if he might climb over at any minute! Use exactly the same principle as on the preceding pages, of dividing the door into 7 in. squares and transferring the pattern from our graph. Instruction No. 4 on the opposite page tells how to decorate walls in a different way, using sticky paper cut-outs. The pattern possibilities for this are endless, of course, so let your imagination go and see what happens!

YOU WILL NEED:
Masking tape
Long rule or plumb line
Soft pencil
Vinyl paints
Large sheets of sticky paper
in various colours

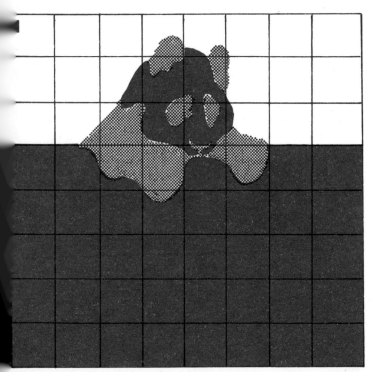

Measure the door. Divide measurement into 7 in. squares. Transfer Panda pattern to graph paper and then on to door. Centre Panda on door and mark 'wall' line to door edges and along side walls. Paint in arms, ears, eyes, nose and mouth detail.

Paint background of door and along wall in pale colour. When dry, stick masking tape along straight edge (on paint).

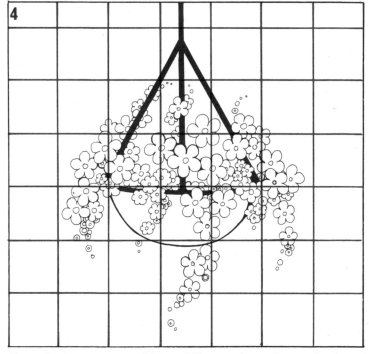

Paint the 'wall' in a bright colour up to masking tape to get a straight edge. Remove tape when all paint is dry.

If you don't trust your painting ability, use large sheets of coloured paper instead. Transfer above pattern to graph paper. Make larger to suit area and cut pattern pieces from large sticky backed paper. Apply to walls, smoothing carefully to ensure flat surface.

Mobiles for Fun

In recent times mobiles have become almost an 'art form' in their own right. It is possible to get mobiles in all sorts of materials and all sorts of shapes. They are, however, extremely expensive to buy and yet, extremely easy to make. Our elegant bird mobile shown above will cost you next to nothing to make and will take you no more than an hour or two—if that! Hang it by a window—it is so light that it will twist and swing in the slightest breeze. Use reversible card as both sides of the birds will show as it turns. The wires we used are available from all craft shops but you could make them yourself by turning up the ends of straight wire with a pair of pliers. Over the page we give instructions for a 'monster' mobile, made initially in one piece and then cut into sections, which each turn gently on their own. Easy and effective! Adapt the design of both ideas using different animal or geometric shapes.

YOU WILL NEED:
For the Bird Mobile
2 pieces of wire 10 in. long
1 piece of wire 6 in. long
Strong thread
3 sheets of different coloured double-sided card (we used white, green, orange)
Self-adhesive paper spots in matching colours
For the 'Monster' Mobile
Stiff card
Coloured foil
Paints
Thread
Piece of wire

Trace and cut out 7 bird bodies (see pattern overleaf) from coloured card. If you follow our colour scheme, you will need 2 green, 2 orange and 3 white.

Trace and cut out wings from card. You will need 3 orange, 3 green and 1 white.

Slash and pierce the body shapes as shown.

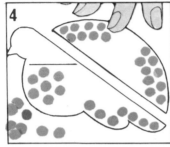

Stick on self adhesive paper spots on body and wings of birds as shown.

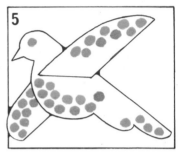

Slot wings through body. If mobile is to hang above eye level slot wings through with patterns showing underneath.

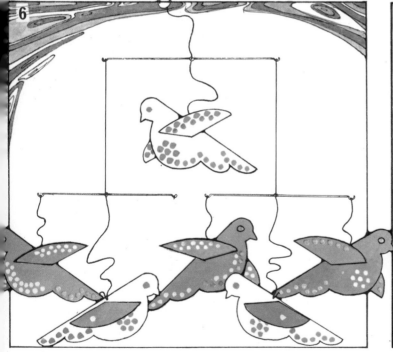

Lay pieces flat to assemble mobile. Thread lengths of string through hole over wings on each bird. Tie one in middle of long wire (leave thread extending above). Tie 2 with equal lengths of thread to ends of long wire, and remaining 4 to ends of short wire.

Suspend mobile from ceiling by wrapping long middle thread round a drawing pin.

1

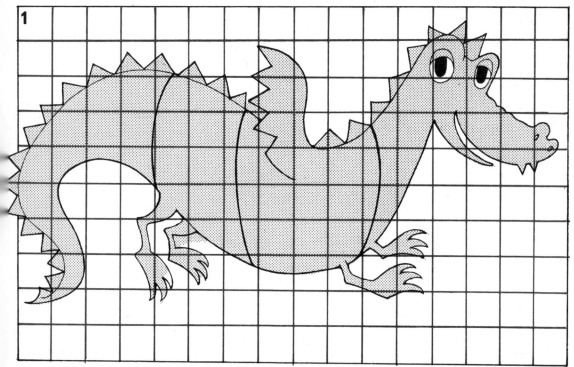

This is a very easy mobile to make and hang, yet it is extremely effective. It is hung from one central piece of wire only. Copy the shape above on to stiff card, using the graph squares to make it as big as you like. Cut out shape, then cut it into four pieces along the lines indicated.

2

Paint each piece adding the appropriate features. Alternatively, cover each piece with coloured foil, smoothing it down well. Paint on features. Cut out scales from foil and glue on.

3

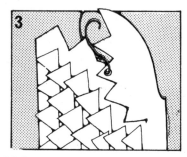

Make a small hole in the top of each piece. Thread through and knot on lengths of string.

4

Cut piece of wire slightly longer than length of monster. Bend it into a shallow curve.

5

Tie each section to wire, so there is a gap of about 1 in. between each. Tie thread to centre of wire and hang from ceiling.

Playtime Spread

Bed-time stories made easy—with this 'adventure' bedspread, which tells a story all by itself! Ours is adapted from the nursery tale of Red Riding Hood, but with the seeds of an idea sown, why not choose something else to 'tell' in the same way? It is also an economical way of making a child's bedspread —we dyed an old sheet and then raided the rag bag for fabric scraps to use for all the shapes. It's an object lesson in not throwing away all those seemingly useless odds and ends of material! Remember to use washable fabrics for everything to avoid disappointment later.

YOU WILL NEED:
Single size white sheet
Cold water dye—blue
Assorted washable fabrics in various colours for animals and other shapes
Seam binding
Wide and narrow ric rac braid
Washable terylene wadding
Assorted cotton and embroidery thread

84

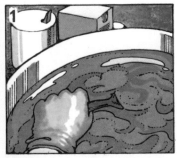

Dye the sheet bright blue using a cold water dye. Follow the maker's instructions printed on the packet.

Trace off the pattern overleaf on to graph paper. Mark outlines with a series of dots.

Transfer pattern to full size by using dressmaker's squared paper or drafting paper. Count position of dots on small pattern and mark off on to large pattern. Join up dots to form shapes.

Trace off pattern of shapes on to large sheets of greaseproof paper and cut out to form pattern templates.

Press sheet and fabric pieces.

Place shapes on fabrics. Cut out allowing $\frac{3}{4}$ in. hem turnings. Also cut out sun, bird, fox's head, owl, trees, ducks, bee's body, mouse, toadstools, squirrel, rabbit and Red Riding Hood shapes in washable wadding.

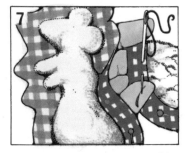

Place wadding on wrong sides of fabric shapes. Turn hem allowance over wadding and tack down firmly.

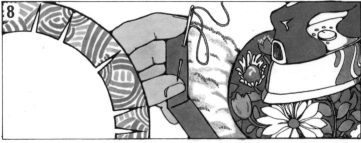

Turn under raw edges of other pieces, snipping turnings where necessary to make smooth curves and sharp points. Tack and press.

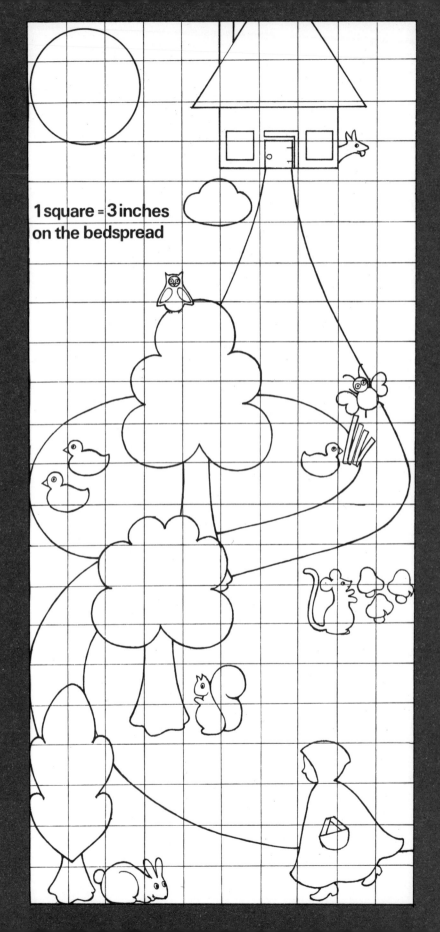

1 square = 3 inches
on the bedspread

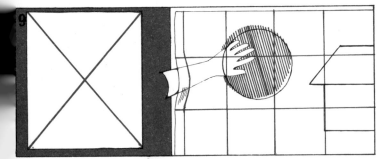

Mark centre of sheet and centre paper pattern on top. Slide footpath, pool and front of house beneath pattern so that they correspond with markings on the paper pattern.

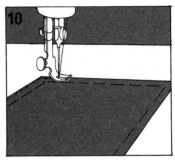

Remove pattern. Pin and tack footpath, pool and house to sheet. Machine round edges with matching thread.

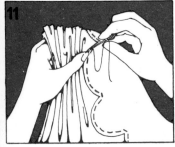

Position trees and clump of flowers. Pin and tack in place. Hemstitch to sheet using tiny firm stitches.

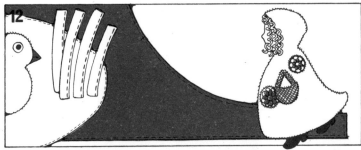

Position and sew on other figures in the same way. Make reeds on pond with folded seam binding. Use narrow ric rac braid for Red Riding Hood's hair. Hem on basket, flowers and boots cut from pieces of fabric.

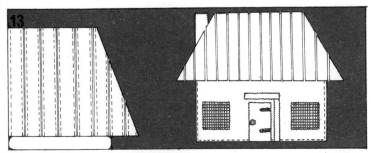

Use wide seam binding stitched on in rows on house to represent thatch. Machine on squares of fabric for doors, windows and chimneys. Embroider door hinges in chain stitch and door knocker in satin stitch.

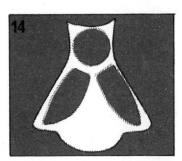

Sew on small scraps of fabric for owl and bee wings, mouse's ears, ducks' bills and squirrel's nuts.

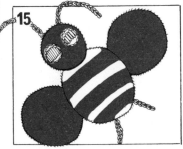

Work embroidery stitches to mark other features such as eyes, whiskers etc.

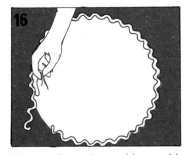

Pin, tack and machine wide ric rac braid round sun and round the edge of the bedspread.

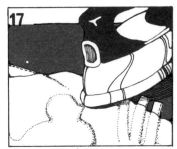

Press background using a damp cloth, using toe of iron around shapes.

Nursery Accessories

An attractive way to use dye is to paint with it. Copy our appealing teddy bear and elephant to make a huge floor cushion and a bed headboard for the nursery. They will both be well received. We give instructions for making the cushion but you could buy a ready-made 36 in. square floor cushion and put in the teddy bear cover. Or you could use the painting idea to create more 'adult' designs, for cushion covers of all sizes, your own personal curtain fabric or table linen or what you will.

YOU WILL NEED:
4 yds. 36 in. wide plain white fabric (natural fabrics such as cotton take the dye best)
Dylon's cold dyes
Cold dye fix
Paintex
Mixing container
Measuring jug
Paint brush
Press studs or zip for cushion and headboard
$\frac{1}{2}$ in. foam 35×25 in.
Cushion filling (kapok or foam off-cuts)
Curtain pole for headboard
3 in. wide white tape

1

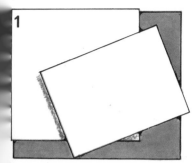

Cut fabric into 2 36 in. squares and 2 oblongs 36 × 26 in. Wash to remove dressing. Dry and iron.

2

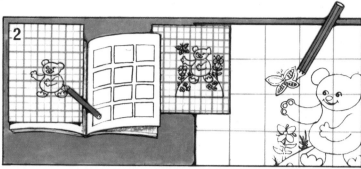

Trace off the patterns overleaf on to graph paper. Transfer to dress-maker's squared paper, upgrading the pattern according to the scale.

3

Trace off the teddy bear pattern on to right side of 1 square fabric shape. Use a soft lead pencil and draw very faint lines.

4

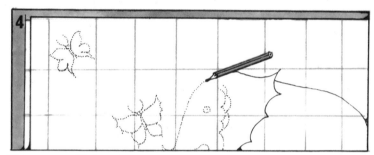

Then trace off the elephant pattern in the same way on to 1 oblong fabric shape.

5

Mix up bowls of each colour dye. Add Paintex, following maker's instructions. Stir.

6

Add the dye fix and stir again. Leave for five minutes, before starting to paint.

7

Lay the square fabric with pattern across a table well covered with clean paper. Then using a paint brush, paint outlines of all shapes first. Then fill in all areas of solid colour.

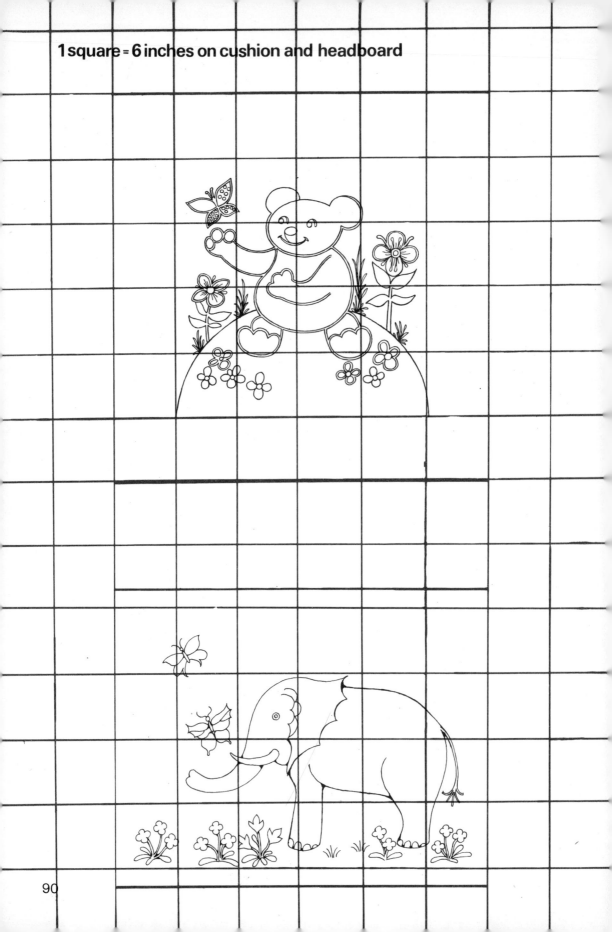

1 square = 6 inches on cushion and headboard

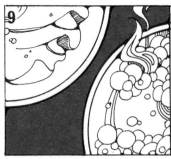

Hang teddy bear pattern up to dry, and paint elephant pattern on oblong material in the same way (i.e. outlines first and then areas of solid colour).

When paint is dry, rinse fabric in cold water and wash in hot soapy water. Rinse. Colours will be fast, and not hard to touch.

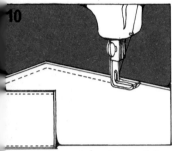

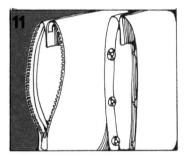

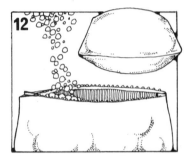

Place right sides of remaining squares of fabric down on teddy bear pattern and machine stitch round 3 sides, $\frac{1}{2}$ in. from edge.

Turn to right side and press. Sew press studs along open edges or sew in a zip.

Make up plain 36 in. square cushion cover and fill with stuffing. Sew edge. Put cushion inside teddy bear cover.

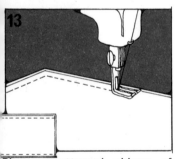

Place unpatterned oblong of fabric on elephant headboard, right sides together and machine sew round three sides, $\frac{1}{2}$ in. from edge.

Turn to right side and press. Sew press studs or zip along the open edge. Insert a piece of $\frac{1}{2}$ in. thick foam the same size as headboard measurements.

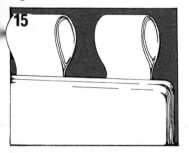

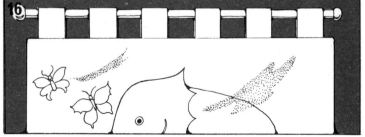

Cut 3 in. wide tapes into 8 in. lengths. Pin, tack and sew firmly at intervals along the top of the headboard.

Slip curtain pole through loops and mount to the wall approximately 2 ft. above the bed.

Book Tidy

Just the thing for books of all sizes and even for small toys. This amusing book rack will provide an incentive for children to put their books tidily away! It's simple to make and effective as you can see. Mount it on a wall, at a height that a small child can reach with ease.

YOU WILL NEED:
¾ yd. deckchair canvas 36 in. wide or similar strong material
3 ft. curtain pole with decorative end stops and brackets
Timber batten 2×1×35 in.
3 applique motifs
3 yds. narrow white ric rac braid
Matching synthetic thread
Glue suitable for fabric
Carpet tacks
3 No. 10 screws and wall plugs
Drill·Pencil
Vinyl paint

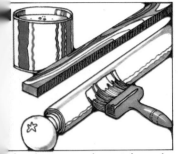

aint batten and curtain pole
ith white vinyl paint. Allow
o dry and apply second coat.

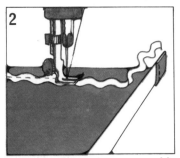

Turn $\frac{1}{2}$ in. hems to wrong side
of fabric along sides and
machine stitch. Stitch ric rac on
seams on right side.

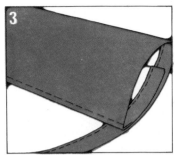

Turn 2 in. of fabric to wrong
side at one end. Machine edge.
Turn over a further 3 in. and
machine to hold curtain pole.

Turn 1$\frac{1}{2}$ in. of fabric to right
side at other end. Press to mark
he line, but do not sew down.

Fold fabric across middle, wrong sides inside and stitch on a row
of braid $\frac{1}{2}$ in. from the bottom on the front of the rack (i.e. side with
deep hem for curtain pole). Position motifs on front and glue in
place.

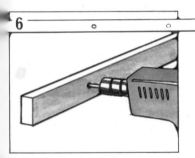

Drill 3 holes in timber batten,
in the centre and 5 in. from either
end.

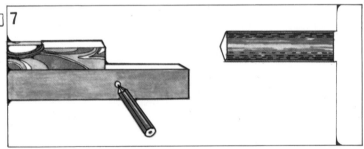

Hold batten to wall at required height and mark wall through holes
with a pencil. (Use a spirit level for a straight line.) Drill and plug
holes using size 10 bit and corresponding plugs.

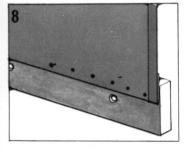

Place wrong side of fabric at
back of rack to back of batten.
Tack in place keeping fabric clear
of screw holes.

Ask someone to hold the canvas clear of the batten while you
screw this to the wall. Mount curtain pole supports level with
the batten at either end. Insert curtain pole into curtain, put on
end stops and hook on to the supports.

Plants in a Bottle

Even the non-greenest fingered person can successfully keep a bottle garden going! Once planted and established, they survive happily for ages needing very little care and attention.

Large glass carboys, like the one pictured, are perhaps the most popular containers for bottle gardens, but they are correspondingly expensive. You can just as effectively use any type of clear glass container which has a neck large enough to insert young plants. Old sweet and pickle jars are ideal, and gardens in goldfish bowls are very attractive too.

Keep your bottle garden in a fairly light position, but out of direct sunlight which will scorch the plants. It needs temperatures that never fall below 50°F to flourish. When first planted keep a watchful eye to see the soil does not dry out, but after a good moisture balance has been established, it will only need watering every 8–12 months. Watch out for discoloured or dying leaves however and nip these off with your pruning knife (see opposite).

YOU WILL NEED:
Large clear glass bottle or carboy (see above)
Broken crocks, or stone chippings and charcoal
Commercial potting compost
Selection of small plants suitable for bottle gardens (see instruction No. 8 overleaf)
6 bamboo canes 2 ft. long
Old kitchen teaspoon, fork and tongs
Razor blade · Old cotton reel
Sellotape

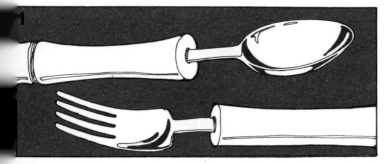

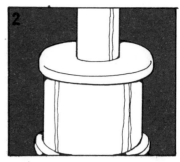

You will need to make some gardening tools for use in your bottle garden. For a 'trowel', cut off handle of old teaspoon and stick end in hollow centre of 2 ft. long bamboo cane. For a 'fork-cum-rake', do the same with an old fork.

Make a 'rammer', (for consolidating soil)—smear end of bamboo with glue and push through centre of spent cotton reel.

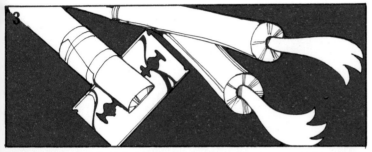

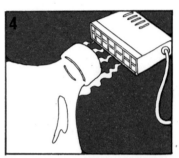

Make a 'pruning knife'—split end of piece of cane, push in a razor blade and fix with Sellotape. For removing cuttings and dead leaves make a pair of long handled tongs, cut off handles of light kitchen tongs and push into 2 ft. bamboo canes.

Wash out carboy thoroughly using lots of soapy water. Leave to dry, (blowing with a hair dryer will help).

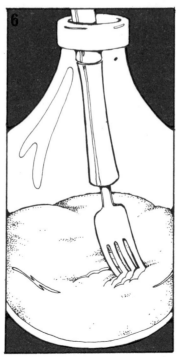

When quite dry, put a layer of washed broken crocks, or stone chippings and charcoal into bottles to provide drainage.

Pour moist commercial potting compost on top to a depth of 4–6 ins. Use fork to make tiny 'hills' and undulations.

Consolidate soil by pushing down firmly with the cotton reel rammer.

8 Choose slow growing plants that are specially recommended for bottle gardens, (your florist or nursery will advise). Use foliage plants not flowering ones—those suitable are *Calatheas, Coces weddelliana,* (dwarf palm), *Cryptanthus bivittatus, Ficus pumila, Fittonia verschaffeltii, Helxine soleirolii, Marantas, Pilea cadierei, Tradescantias.*

9 Try out a few arrangements of the plants before planting to see how they look most effective.

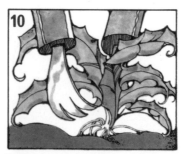

10 Plant at edges first. Make a hole in compost with 'trowel'. Drop in first plant (roots first). Manoeuvre with 'tongs'.

11 Cover the roots with soil using 'trowel' and then firm the soil using the cotton reel 'rammer'.

12 Repeat with all plants, planting towards centre. Do not squash against sides of bottle—(a few leaves can touch edges).

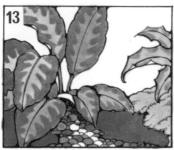

13 Add interest by covering parts of the soil with stones or pieces of moss.

16 Close up top of bottle. At first it will steam up with condensation, but this will soon clear.

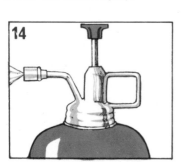

14 Water plants using a small cylindrical garden spray with nozzle set at an angle. Wash off any soil adhering to leaves.

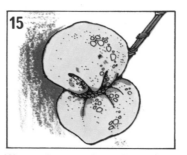

15 Wrap wire round small sponge. Moisten it and clean up inside of bottle so no soil remains adhering to edges.